# Mumbai 26/11
## Security Imperatives For The Future

# Mumbai 26/11

## Security Imperatives For The Future

Brig Rahul K. Bhonsle (Retd)

## Vij Books

4675-A, 21 Ansari Road, Darya Ganj
New Delhi-110002

Published  by

## Vij Books

(Publishers, Distributors & Importers)
4675-A, 21 Ansari Road
New Delhi - 110002
Phones: 91-11-65449971, 91-11- 43596460
Fax: 91-11-30126465
web  : www.vanishbooks.com
e-mail  : vijbooks@rediffmail.com


Copyright © author, 2009


ISBN 10 : 81-904285-9-4
ISBN 13 : 978-81-904285-9-0

 (Library Edition of this book is also available)

Price   :  Rs 295.00

Printed in India
at Narula Printers, Delhi

Cover Design by Vision Impact

*Dedicated to the Mumbaikar, whose voices of protests have shaken the conscience of the power elites in New Delhi and to those brave hearts who laid down their lives fighting the dastardly act of terror.*

# Contents

# Preface

## Maximum Metro, Murderous Mayhem

Reflection over an event which has happened a month ago may not provide accurate perspectives for the future. Yet in the times in which we live, with two nuclear armed neighbours, India and Pakistan on the brink of war or the next terror strike just a moment away, a swift appraisal of events gone by is essential to show the light to a saner course ahead. This book is an attempt towards the same, how so ever imperfect it may seem to the purists, if it breaks through the, "stability-instability" paradox in the Sub Continent the effort may be worth it.

Ironically the truth is well known to both sides. Pakistan's government and the people know that it is the hub of terrorism in South Asia, a condition of its own making, the details of which need not be gone into here. India's debility against terror be it intelligence, operational or judicial is also self inflicted. Despite clear indications of growing threat of terror from Pakistan as well from forces within, the governments over the years in New Delhi have preferred the route of avoidance. The Ostrich approach is perhaps a legacy of the Partition shared by both New Delhi and Islamabad.

Simplistically the solution too is obvious; the first step is shedding off denial. India seems to have accepted the challenge of countering terrorism and has at long last set about implementing measures under a result oriented Home Minister, Mr P Chidambaram. However for a large complex democracy with a federal structure, where basic governance is either non existent or sabotaged by the nexus of politician-criminal and contractor, delivering the objective of zero tolerance for terrorism will not be easy.

In Pakistan the story is somewhat different. The political government, the people and opinion makers accept that non state actors and terrorist groups are an existential threat to the country. Yet the strategic space controlled by what is known as the Establishment comprising of the Army and the Inter Services Intelligence is engaged in an exercise of denial and diversion. Overlooking the 'caliphates' and 'emirates' springing up in FATA and NWFP under leaders as Mangal Bagh and Baitullah Mehsud whose focus is shifting from Afghanistan to Pakistan and vice versa, troop redeployment is taking place to the Eastern borders with India. The Establishment has refused to acknowledge that Kasab, the lone terrorist apprehended in Mumbai is from the country, even though his own father has declared him to be his son.

The peripatetic External Affairs Minister of India Mr Pranab Mukherjee who is in the forefront of the Indian diplomatic offensive against Islamabad is driven to his wits end by such stonewalling tactics. With the experience of a previous occasion when India mobilized troops for a year in 2002 in an Operation which lasted for almost a year but failed to attain the desired objective of neutralizing the threat of terror from Pakistan, Mukherjee wanted to think differently, but is so far stymied by Islamabad's response which many believe is driven by the chain smoking, soft spoken Army Chief, Kayani the very anti thesis of his predecessor, blustering Pervez Musharraf.

Here again the options before Islamabad are simple but denial of the threat posed by religious extremism and militancy to internal order and stability as much as to India has only highlighted the government's lack of will and inability to control self destruction. Pakistan needs international support to put its economic house in order, as well as to cope with the difficult internal and external security situation. Thus control of extremism within and peace with India is a sine qua nan to Pakistan's anti militancy strategy. Ironically the ruling elite have decided to do just the opposite.

Thus the strategic Catch 22 of increased uneasiness in India that Pakistan is not doing enough and the canard by Pakistan that enough evidence has not been provided by New Delhi has led to a stalemate at least as we turn the leaf into the New Year, 2009.

On the positive side the Taj Mahal Tower and Trident Hotels in Mumbai, symbols of the 26/11 terror attack on India's commercial capital opened on 21 December, even before a month passed by. The Leopold Café had opened on the fourth day, markers of resilience of the people of Mumbai as well as a reminder to the terrorist groups that attention span of their dastardly acts lasts but a few hours and days in the public mind space.

Given this backdrop, this perspective on Mumbai 26/11 attempts to draw lessons for the future. In Chapter 2 we look at the terror attack and the counter terror operation that lasted for 60 long hours, admire the resolve of the Mumbaikar who struck back within days in Chapter 3 and draw contours of the Lashkar e Taiyyaba, the group behind the strike in Chapter 4. In Chapter 5 we move on to review the Indian response, the diplomatic power play in Chapter 6 and visualize an Indo Pakistan escalation and de-escalation matrix in Chapter 7. In Chapter 8, the possibilities of Pakistan dismantling the terrorist infrastructure are analysed ending with suggestions for implementing the lessons from Mumbai focused on three key issues operationalising intelligence, border and marine security and police capability building in Chapter 9.

The lessons learnt and suggestions made are not by any chance brilliant momentary insights from Mumbai but thoughts on countering terrorism distilled by the many hours of discussions in seminars, informal chats and bar room strategizing over the years. While any flaws are singularly mine, the credit for the pearls of wisdom if any goes to my numerous colleagues, philosophers, guides and friends who for fear of injustice to those who I may miss out, have taken the liberty of not including here. If the kudos come I will make an endeavor to share the same personally when we meet next.

A word of thanks to Rohan Vij, the young publisher of Vij Books with enormous stakes in the well being of India, who has made this book possible in the time that it ought to have been published, just a month after, Mumbai 26/11.

This book is dedicated to the Mumbaikar, whose voices of protests have shaken the conscience of the power elites in New Delhi. We hope and pray that they display a similar resolve as the citizen of Mumbai for a terror free Mumbai and India.

New Delhi

28 December 2008                                        Rahul K Bhonsle

# Mumbai 26/11
# Multiple Effects, New Wave Terror

*"On behalf of the Government, I would like to apologise to our people for the fact that those dastardly acts could not be prevented".*

Indian Prime Minister Manmohan Singh in Parliament,
11 December 2008

## Introduction

Multiple terror attacks struck Mumbai, India's financial capital on the night of 26 November. A shocked nation was paralysed by a series of simultaneous assaults in South Mumbai, traditional hub of the metropolis at a time when revellers were out on the streets and the common man was preparing to go to bed. Many realized that Mumbai had been struck only when they got up in the wee hours of 27 November to learn that schools and offices were closed for the day. These attacks in the heart of Mumbai in the proximity of the Gateway of India were seen by the nation as an assault on Indian sovereignty much in the same vein of the parliamentary strike in December 2001.The sheer audacity and roving fire power created impact of much larger numbers leading the Chief Minister of Maharashtra to indicate at one time that there were 20-25 men who had struck the state capital. The Mumbai police later confirmed that there were only 10 terrorists.[1] 179 persons, including 26 foreigners lost their lives while 296 persons including 22 foreigners suffered injuries in the attack, planned to kill and maim as many people as possible.[2] Police investigator Rakesh Maria indicated based on interrogation of the captured terrorist that the plan was to kill maximum people, "What we have learned from Kasab is they were told: open random fire, kill as many people as you can, take hostages, then go to a vantage location and stay put," said Maria. It was a sad reminder of lack of preparedness of India's premier city to face a terror assault despite many prior warnings.

Speaking at the UN Security Council on Threats to International Peace and Security Caused by Terrorist Acts on 9 December, India's Minister of State for External Affairs Mr. E. Ahamed, recounted the horrific tragedy thus, "A group of ten terrorists from the global terrorist organization Lashkar-e-Toiba reached Mumbai in the evening of 26th November 2008. The group divided themselves into four smaller groups and proceeded to pre-selected targets which included a café, popular with Indian and foreign tourists and two major hotels. Each terrorist was armed and equipped with AK rifles, pistols, grenades, explosives and communications. The terrorist attack was conducted like a commando operation indicating that the perpetrators had received professional training both generally as well as specifically regarding this attack itself. They were indoctrinated with ruthlessness and barbarity – innocent passengers including women and children were indiscriminately sprayed with bullets at the railway station and public places; hostages were taken in the hotels who were subsequently massacred. It is significant that this was the first terrorist attack in India where foreigners were specifically segregated and targeted". [3]

He went on to add that nine terrorists were killed in the action taken by security forces while one of them was apprehended. His interrogation revealed that they were trained in Pakistan and were launched from a ship from Karachi. They traveled into Indian waters, took control of an Indian boat, killing the crew. Thereafter, they came to Mumbai to cause mayhem and murder. [4]

The Mumbai attack is classified by many as a sophisticated "commando" terror operation the likes of which has not been seen in the past except for an aborted plot, planned by the Al Qaeda on Manhattan in 1993, which had signatures of what happened in Mumbai on 26 July.[5] The key facets of the attack on 26 November which extended till all terrorists were killed on 29 November can be briefly broken down in the following main stages[6]:-

- The terror group approached Mumbai from the sea hijacking one of the fishing trawlers, a large number of which operate in the waters between India and Pakistan particularly from the Gujarat coast.
- The group comprising of 10 terrorists landed on the Mumbai coast in a rubber dinghy, disembarking from the trawler about 20 nautical miles off shore.
- The group split in five teams of two terrorists each and fanned out in the city striking first at the Leopold Café and Chhatrapati Shiyaji Terminal (CST) firing indiscriminately, throwing grenades and generally creating mayhem.
- One team was intercepted and a terrorist was killed and

one apprehended. However the initial onslaught saw a number of civilian deaths, while the Mumbai police suffered the loss of its key officers including the anti terror squad chief. Ten bombs were also planted with timers, two of which exploded in taxis, while others were defused.

• The four teams left, moved to three predetermined targets, the Taj Hotel, Oberoi Trident Hotel and Nariman House, base of an ultra orthodox Jewish group.

• At these sites they again fired indiscriminately, held hostages but by this time were effectively surrounded by the police and Rapid Action Force.

• A rescue operation was launched by the Marine Commandoes followed by the specialist counter terrorist organisation the, National Security Guards (NSG) flown in from New Delhi which lasted almost 60 hours and eliminated all four terrorist teams.

• The death toll rose to 179 with several injured by the time the operation was called off.

A post strike survey reconstructed from inputs by intelligence agencies through the media and statement of the Minister of State for External Affairs in the UN Security Council revealed that the attack was launched by the Lashkar e Taiyyaba; a group linked to the Al Qaeda, based in Pakistan. The Lashkar is known to be antagonistic towards India and envisages fundamentalist Salafist rule across the region. This was also the first attack in India replicating global terror with attackers coming in from the sea, targeting hotels frequented by foreigners and taking on a fundamental Jewish establishment. Sadly but surely India has arrived on the international terrorism scene.

The glaring inadequacies of the Indian state were far too apparent to be ignored particularly so when the people of Mumbai came on the streets rejecting the political class in one voice while the ever vigilant media, reflecting the sullen mood of the people. Public anger led to the removal (couched as resignation) of the Home Minister of the country as well as the Maharashtra state and the Chief minister of the latter. An overhaul of the security mechanism is underway and it is hoped that a repeat of Mumbai may not come about.

On the regional and the international plane with clear indications of involvement of terrorist groups based in Pakistan, the question was to what degree the Pakistan government, the army and Inter Services Intelligence (ISI) were involved. The Indian government capitalized on the capture of the single terrorist, "Kasab" alive and established proof of involvement of Pakistani citizens leading that country to clamp down on at least one camp in the Pakistan Occupied Kashmir by 9 December 2008. India also recommended a ban on the Jamaat Ud Dawa (JuD) parent organisation of the Lashkar to the UN Security Council Committee established pursuant to paragraph 6 of resolution 1267 (1999) concerning Al-Qaida and the Taliban and associated individuals and entities on 9 December.[7] The UN Security Council accepted India's position and the JuD, Al Rashid Trust and Al Akhtar Trust International along with four individuals including Hafiz Muhammad Saeed were added to the Consolidated List imposing sanctions on the individuals and organisations.[8]

The Indo Pakistan standoff, with the United States acting as an intermediary lest the two cross the nuclear red lines, is continuing. India accuses Pakistan of denying involvement of its citizens in the terror attack, while Islamabad is harping on the fact that no credible evidence has been provided. The rhetoric is increasing in bitterness each day. The Indian side presented to the Pakistani Deputy High Commissioner, the confessional statement of the lone terrorist apprehended Kasab, which the Pakistani's media has rejected as this was not admissible in law.[9] Meanwhile the political battle is taking new shape in Islamabad, with former Prime Minister Nawaz Sharif asking why Kasab's village, Faridkot in Punjab has been cordoned off. In the typically surcharged atmosphere, Indian media claimed this as Nawaz Sharif accepting that Kasab was a Pakistani adding fuel to the fire.

The newly anointed Home Minister in India, Shri P. Chidambaram announced a slew of measures to enhance security and check terrorism and insurgency. These included establishment of a Coastal Command, adoption of National Investigation Agency Act, creating National Security Guards Hubs and allocation of additional funds for police modernization. He also commenced daily briefings from the intelligence heads perhaps for the first time after many years where the National Security Advisor was also present. In the short term these measures added to the confidence of the masses and there is a sense of greater purpose seen in actions of the Home Ministry after a long time to combat terrorism.

The citizens of Mumbai after the initial shock of terror were quickly recuperating from the distress. Leopold Café in Colaba was the first to get off the blocks opening within days of the strike. Ratan Tata and the Oberoi's opened The Taj and Trident respectively on 21 December 2008, even before a month was to lapse after the terror attack. The poignant visitors to the hotels paid a tribute to the sacrifice of a large number of hotel employees in the line of duty before filling up the tables for the evening. Security was obviously tight and police and barricades were seen everywhere, shutting the door after the terrorists had bolted some would say but as the old proverb goes, it is never too late. Many across the nation shocked by images of smoke billowing out of the Taj heaved a sigh of relief to see the tables filling up in the cafes as well as in neighbouring Trident. The citizen had certainly got better of the terrorist.

While the attacks were aimed at the ex patriates and foreign nationals visiting Mumbai, they accepted this stoically. "Certainly it's gotten our attention that up to this point the terrorist attacks in India have been random and not organized toward westerners. It's made a difference in our thinking," said Philip Rynearson, an American elementary school teacher who has been living and working in Delhi for four months. He added, "I don't think there's much you can really do to plan for things like this. You just have to live your life and maybe be a little more aware. I don't see us making any drastic changes." Here again the larger aim of the terrorists to drive in fear in foreign nationals seems to have been overwhelmingly defeated.[10]

For the Indian and Pakistani governments defending their own positions mostly through the media, talking at each other rather than to each other, "all options" remained open. There was much jingoism over being prepared for any and every eventuality with allegations of crossing the International Border by the Indian

Air Force by Pakistani authorities, which was hotly denied. This was preceded by a fake call received by President Zardari allegedly from External Affairs Minister, Mr Pranab Mukherjee, threatening war leading to scrambling of the Pakistani Air Force. The dust over these issues has yet to settle down as both sides prepare to achiever their aims through confronting each other rather than jointly facing the challenge emanating from terrorist groups as the Lashkar who have survived through support in parts of the Pakistani establishment as well as amongst the hard line religious lobbies who have been vocal over the past few days raising their voices even against the United Nations.

Over a period of one month, the full gamut of escalation, de-escalation and re-escalation has been gone through by both the countries. The Indian position was explained most succinctly by the External Affairs Minister Mr Pranab Mukherjee who appeared to be once again the government's point man in a crisis. Addressing Heads of Mission on 22 December in New Delhi in the first ever conclave of such nature where over 120 mission chiefs were present, Mr Pranab Mukherjee while underlining the achievements of his Ministry over the past four years of the Congress rule highlighted that relations with Pakistan had not progressed positively. Making specific reference to the Mumbai terror attacks and engagement of Pakistan he stated, "We have so far worked at several levels. At the international level we have sought the support of the international community to put pressure on Pakistan to deal effectively with the terrorism. We have highlighted that the infrastructure of terrorism in Pakistan has to be dismantled permanently. We are not saying this just because we are affected but because we believe that it will be good for the entire world and also for Pakistani people and society". [11]

The same day as Mr Mukherjee spoke, 22 December Pakistan Air Force (PAF) fighter jets flew several times over Islamabad, Rawalpindi, Lahore and other cities. "In view of current environment, PAF has enhanced its vigilance," said a statement attributed to the PAF. The forward bases of PAF at Lahore, Sargodha and Chaklala were also put on high alert.[12] The Defence Minister Ahmad Mukhtar Chaudhry of the country also indicated most ominously that, "If India tried to thrust war, then the armed forces of Pakistan have all the potential and right to defend (the country), if it breaks out, then god forbid the situation might develop into a nuclear war." The US Joint Chiefs of Staff, Mr Mike Mullens was in Islamabad, for the second time in a month, the first being on 3 December.[13] The two sides of diplomacy, brinkmanship and conflict diffusion were operating at high speed, when the Indian Prime Minister stated on 23 December, that war is not a solution. All this left the common man as well as the security analyst guessing as to which way the countries were headed.

The Mumbai terror attacks have thus created a strategic hiatus and are much more than an ordinary strike; it was an assault with multiple aims and effects, some intended by the attackers, others possibly inadvertent and never envisaged. The impact was felt on the political situation in Pakistan, affected the regional balance in South Asia and also threatened the war in Afghanistan being waged by the international community at large. In the first month at least, the group seems to have achieved its aim of causing anarchy in the corridors of power in the Sub Continent. While

contours of the attack are now reasonably clear and the
perpetrators identified, their motives and manifestations need
further analysis. More over this is possibly the first multiple
impulse attack in India denoting a new wave in global terrorism.
Thus a detailed review of the tragedy of Mumbai 26/11 is necessary.

**(Endnotes)**

1 Indian Police Arrest 2 in Mumbai Investigation and Look at Cell phone
Link. New York Tims Report. Available at http://www.nytimes.com/2008/
12/07/world/asia/07mumbai.html?ref=asia

2 Statement by Mr. E. Ahamed, Minister of State for External Affairs at
the UN Security Council on Threats to International Peace and Security
Caused by Terrorist Acts. Available at MEA India.nic.in.

3 Ibid

4 Ibid

5 Fred Burton and Ben West, in Stratfor.com report, "From the New York
Landmarks Plot to the Mumbai Attack". Report shared by email to the
author by Stratfor.com

6 Details of the operation have been recreated from reports appearing in
the media and Statement of the Indian Home Minister in the Parliament
on 11 December 2008. Security-risks.com does not authenticate media
reports.

7 Ibid

8 Security Council Al Qaida and Taliban Sanctions Committee Adds
Names of Four Individuals to Consolidated List, Amends Entries of Three
Entities. Available at http://www.un.org/News/Press/docs/2008/
sc9527.doc.htm

9 Statement of Pakistani Daily Dawn Editor Ayaz Amir on CNN IBN on
22 December 2008 in 9 O'Clock News. 2130, 22 December.

10 Jessica Thompson.Foreigners unfazed in Delhi after Mumbai attacks.

Available    at    http://timesofindia.indiatimes.com/Cities/
Foreigners_unfazed_in_Delhi/articleshow/3780317.cms
11 Inaugural Address by External Affairs Minister Shri Pranab Mukherjee
at Heads of Missions Conference (22-24 December 2008, New Delhi).
Available at http://meaindia.nic.in/
12 PAF increases aerial surveillance. Daily Times Report 23 December
2008.    Available    at    http://www.dailytimes.com.pk/
default.asp?page=2008\12\23\story_23-12-2008_pg1_1
13 Rumours of war create panic in Pakistan. Economic Times Report. 23
December 2008. Avaialble at http://economictimes.indiatimes.com/News/
PoliticsNation/Rumours_of_war_create_panic_in_Pakistan/articleshow/
3875617.cms

# 2

# The Terror Strike and the Counter Terror Operation

*"We tried to capture the terrorists alive. But the kind of resistance they offered gave us no choice but to kill them. We had given them enough warnings to surrender."*

Director General National Security Guards Mr. J K Dutt

Operationally the Mumbai terror attack has been likened to a conventional special forces raid having classic characteristics generally associated with highly trained regular forces. Thus it had a most difficult and unconventional approach, multiple targets, and asymmetric impact, dislocation of the victim's command and control and an overall strategic effect. The key difference being that it was a cowardly strike on defenceless men and women on the street, people returning home from a hard days work by local trains, socialites enjoying a dinner and businessmen savouring an aperitif after a long day, something which a regular force would never undertake. Despite the high level of casualties, the attack failed to make a larger impact, for the feeling of fear was to last for a very short period, a week or more, as Mumbai came back on its feet with the Taj and Trident opening on 22 December, just before Christmas eve.

Broadly as indicated by Mr P Chidambaram in the Indian Parliament, 10 Pakistani nationals belonging to the Lashkar-e-Toiba, a proscribed terrorist outfit left Karachi on November 23, 2008 and boarded a launch by the name of Al Hussaini. They accosted and hijacked an Indian fishing vessel, M. V. Kuber, off the coast of Gujarat; killed its occupants; and a few miles short of the coast of Mumbai abandoned the fishing vessel, got into an inflatable rubber dinghy, and landed near Budhwar Park, Colaba, Mumbai between 8.00 p.m. and 8.30 p.m. on November 26, 2008. The terrorists split into four to five groups with targets being C' atrapati Shivaji Terminus (CST); the Leopold Café and Taj Hotel; the Oberoi – Trident Hotel and the Nariman House. These attacks involved indiscriminate firing, throwing of grenades and bomb blasts at 13 locations. [1] This account roughly matches the confessional statement of the terrorist apprehended, Ajmal included at Appendix A. The strike caused panic and mayhem for over three nights in India's commercial capital, with schools and offices remaining closed. The details of the multiple terror strike and the counter terror operation would thus provide important lessons for the future.

## The Maritime Approach

Recreating the entire episode it is evident that the terror group started from Karachi on the Al Hussaini, with the intent of boarding a fishing vessel en route. This was not unusual as a large number of fishing boats from India are in these waters and fishermen from both sides are known to encroach in each others areas from time to time. Switching over to a fishing vessel was essential to avoid detection by the Indian Coast Guard. These fears of the group proved ominous, with the Coast Guard launching operations to locate Al Hussaini based on intelligence inputs, but by then they had probably shifted to the fishing vessel, the M V Alpha Kuber, presumably commandeered in the waters between India and Pakistan.

The Alpha Kuber was later intercepted by the Indian Coast Guard 112 km from the Mumbai coast and investigations led to confirmation of its involvement in the strike.[2] The owner of the Kuber was in touch with his crew till 21 November but thereafter lost contact. New revelations indicated possible involvement of the ship in providing support to the terrorist group but these have been ruled out for now. "While the terrorists were travelling in Kuber they had distributed their duties like standing on the watch tower to keep surveillance, keeping tabs on the activity of the navigator so that he could not alert the navy authorities, etc. A diary, containing details of two-hourly duty distribution, has been seized," Rakesh Maria chief investigator of Mumbai police indicated later.

Shifting from M V Alpha Kuber about 20 nautical miles off the Mumbai coast, the group travelled in one rubber dinghy alighting at the jetty off Badhwar Park, Colaba, which normally has heavy boat traffic varying at any time up to 2000 boats.[3&4] They used Gemini inflatable boats with a 20 HP engine of Yamaha make with engine and chassis numbers erased. Most likely it was a medium sized Gemini inflatable dinghy which as per the British Admiralty Manual of Seamanship of 1995 can carry, 9 plus 2 crew.[5] The passengers of the boat when questioned by the locals showed weapons and said, "We are under tension" as per a report in the

Times of India.[6] The landing was corroborated by two witnesses a guest staying in the Taj Hotel and fishermen who were in the nearby colony.[7] At the jetty in Badhwar Park, the attackers reportedly split in five groups of two each and commandeered vehicles to strike at the Leopold Café and the Chhatrapati Shivaji Terminus (CST).

## The CST and Leopold Café

Chhatrapati Shivaji Terminus is the headquarters of the Central Railways. It is one of the busiest railway stations in India serving main as well as suburban passengers.[8] The station building is designed in a mix of Victorian and Gothic style of architecture and is a World heritage site. Known as Victoria Terminus or VT before, it was symbolic as a destination for the great Indian dream for thousands of youth who thronged to Mumbai in search of jobs over the decades. Sadly two men choose to shatter the serenity with their automatic guns and grenades.

The Leopold Café open since 1871, boasts of the best chicken tikka in town and is a favourite sit out for travelers, tourists and the young of Mumbai alike. Once again a icon of Mumbai's free spirit, cosmopolitan culture and old world charm, it would be anathema to an extremist seeped in a culture of violent divisiveness.

The first attack came on the Leopold Café at about 2130 hours (IST). Two terrorists sprayed bullets in the premises killing many and then made their way towards Hotel Taj. The terrorists stayed at the Leopold Café only for a short while, thus there was no response from the security forces to confront them. Another pair attacked the CST at about the same time as the Leopold Café and sprayed bullets in identical fashion killing 48. They faced limited resistance and it was presence of mind of the announcer at the booth which ensured that the Station was quickly evacuated thereby preventing further losses. After the CST attack, the terrorists were at a loss as to what they should do and thus moved towards Cama Hospital at about 22:59 hrs, reached GT Hospital at 23:19 hrs and Head Office Gate No. 6 at 00:07 hrs continuing to spray bullets enroute.[9] From Cama hospital they moved in a police Qualis after killing the occupants, ATS Joint Commissioner of Police Hemant Karkare, Additional Commissioner of Police Ashok Kamte and encounter specialist Vijay Salaskar.[10] The two commandeered a Skoda when the Toyota Qualis was shot up in the tyres. At Girgaum Chowpatty they were intercepted by the police and one of the terrorist Ismail was killed while another later identified as "Kasab" was apprehended.[11]

Recounting the operation at the CST, the Home Minister stated in the Parliament, "security personnel belonging to the Mumbai police and the RPF confronted the two heavily armed terrorists. After causing mayhem at CST, the two terrorists escaped via a lane opposite the station. Meanwhile, as soon as news of the firing at the CST and near Cama Hospital was received, police officers rushed to the sites. There was an unexpected – and fortuitous – confrontation between the two terrorists and the police personnel in which three officers were killed. Subsequently, the two terrorists were challenged by a police party and, in an exchange of fire, one terrorist was killed and one was captured alive. The name of the apprehended terrorist is Mohammed Ajmal

Amir. Interrogation and investigation have revealed that he belongs to Village Faridkot , in District Ukada, in the province of Punjab in Pakistan". [12]

The Indian Express has provided another graphic account of the encounter at the CST. The duo of Ismail Khan and Kasab led by the former is stated to have entered the station around 9.30 PM and started firing randomly at the passengers inside the station. When cornered by the police they took position behind a railway coach and engaged the policemen in a gun battle, lobbing grenades before they managed to escape towards the Cama hospital. Karkare, Kamte and Salaskar, Mumbai's three brave police officers arrived in the lane almost simultaneously. Seeing the police Qualis the terrorists opened fired and killed the three officers instantaneously such was the intensity of the firing. Pulling out the bodies, they sat in the vehicle and moved towards the Vidhan Bhawan. Here they had a flat tyre and then commandeered a white Skoda and sped towards Marine Drive. At Girgaum Chowpatty around 12.30 AM past midnight they were intercepted at a police barrier. In the encounter that followed, Khan and a brave police inspector, Tukaram Omble was killed while Kasab was caught alive.[13] This proved to be prize catch for the Mumbai police as he sung and placed Pakistani authorities in an extremely embarrassing situation back home. Kasab's citizenship would be a major bone of contention in the days ahead.

## The Taj Hotel

The Taj Hotel is one of the eternal attractions of Mumbai. Built in 1903, much before the Gateway of India, the Hotel's web site describes its ambience best thus, "__an architectural marvel and brings together Moorish, Oriental and Florentine styles. Offering panoramic views of the Arabian Sea and the Gateway of India, the hotel is a gracious landmark of the city of Mumbai, showcasing contemporary Indian influences along with beautiful vaulted alabaster ceilings, onyx columns, graceful archways, hand-woven silk carpets, crystal chandeliers, a magnificent art collection, an eclectic collection of furniture, and a dramatic cantilever stairway".  The Taj is more than a.hotel; it is an art gallery, a meeting place for socialites, an architectural wonder as well as a historical iconic structure. The hotel has 565 rooms which generated revenues worth Rs 400 Crore in 2007-08, while the Trident has 575 rooms.[14] Frequented by foreign as well as Indian guests, the Taj was a symbol of Mumbai's free spirit as well as opulence, an ideal target for suicide terrorists.

The group which attacked the Leopold Café made their way to the Taj Mahal hotel. At the Taj Hotel, they lobbed grenades in the Hotel's swimming pool and sprayed gun fire and started taking hostages particularly of foreign nationality, killing people at random.[15] As per an escapee Mr Rakesh Patel a businessman from London who lives in Hong Kong they were youth in their 20's. Rakesh Patel said, "The two young boys came to the restaurant and took us upstairs. We were taken to the 18th floor from where we escaped".[16] This group was later reportedly joined by two more gunmen, who all entered the Taj Hotel from the rear door given that there were security checks in the front and even if they had killed the security guards, the alarm raised would have led to people inside escaping their dragnet.

The police are reported to have continuously intercepted the cell phone conversations of the terrorists to their Karachi boss, known as Amir. A total of eight conversations were reported from the terrorists in the Taj and three from Nariman House. The terrorists in the Taj were instructed, "Hotel mein aag laga do. Jab public bhaage gi, tum escape kar lena (burn the hotel and escape when the public panics).[17]

The National Security Guards (NSG) counter terror operation was started with 14 commandoes entering the Taj first and which started clearing the premises room by room from the top. They first covered the sixth and fifth floors and were heading to the fourth floor when they got information of three terrorists in red, blue and green T shirts in room number 471. They used the master key to open the door asking the terrorists to surrender but were fired at by the terrorists and during the encounter Major Sandeep Unnikrishnan of the NSG was killed.[18] The NSG saw that the terrorists had brought in large quantities of ammunition and hand grenades perhaps due to which rumours were floated during the siege that they had stocked Taj with ammunition before hand. They also stated that the terrorists seemed to be familiar with the layout of the hotel well and kept firing, throwing grenades and disappearing in the corridors.[19]

### The Oberoi Trident

The Oberoi Trident is even bigger than the Taj Mahal hotel with 575 rooms (547 post strike as per the Hotels web site).[20] The Hotel claims to offer the, "best view of Mumbai – The Marine Drive, a 3-kms-long beautiful promenade that rings a natural

bay, greets guests at the Trident, Nariman Point". The towering
structure distinctly stands out of the Mumbai skyline and is
popular, "being located in the heart of the financial and business
district with access to major corporate houses, entertainment,
recreation and shopping centres".[21]

A third pair of terrorists had made its way to the Hotel
and took many hostages moving up the higher floors of the hotel
to deter rescue by the police.[22] The two terrorists in Oberoi Hotel
sealed the restaurants Tiffin and Banquet room and took hostages,
moving from room to room they opened fire indiscriminately.
The hostage episode in the hotel continued for hours. One of the
terrorists made a call to India TV using cell phone of a Swedish
tourist in Room No. 1856, saying, "We demand the release of all
mujaheddin put in jails. Then will we release these people.
Otherwise, we will destroy this place. . . . You must have seen
what's happening here." On being asked by the television station,
"Do you have the single demand that all mujaheddin arrested be
released . . . or do you have any other demand?" this terrorist
identified as Shadullah responded, "Yes, release them, and we,
the Muslims who live in India, should not be harassed . . . Things
like demolition of Babri Masjid and killings should stop."[23] In what
is seen as a review of earlier policy, the Indian government refused
to negotiate with the terrorists.

At the Oberoi Trident, the NSG stormed the hotel from
the 21st storey roof top rescuing hotels as they went from floor to
floor. Here with water from fire fighters filling the floors clearance
was even more complicated, but the NSG in a 41 hours operation
succeeded in clearing the premises floor by floor. The NSG

commandoes attempted to catch more terrorists alive. As the Director General Mr. J K Dutt stated in a briefing during the operation, "We tried to capture the terrorists alive. But the kind of resistance they offered gave us no choice but to kill them. We had given them enough warnings to surrender."[24] The clearing operation was extremely slow and time consuming. "We had to make sure that each and every room was cleared before we proceeded to secure an upper floor. This proved to be very time consuming," said NSG Chief J K Dutt confirming that approximately 200 commandoes were part of the overall operation.[25] Trident was cleared by the NSG before the Taj, with only two terrorists reported there.

## Nariman House

Nariman House also known as Chabad House is the base in Mumbai of an orthodox Jewish group named Chabad Lubavitch of Brooklyn, New York. A number of Israeli tourists and others gather there in the evening for kosher food. Two terrorists approached Nariman house. Here the main intent was to take hostages. Given the Jewish background of the people held, the message was clear. The hostages were all held on the third floor and the bodies of the Rabbi Gavriel Holtzberg and his wife Rivka were found there, while the terrorists having killed them made their way to the top floor. [26] There was enough evidence that the Holzbergs were brutally treated along with the other hostages. [27]

Rabi Taub who came from New York to ensure that no autopsy was conducted on the bodies of the Jews as per religious strictures was sure that the Nariman House attack was a deliberate attempt to target the orthodox community, "No one neither the police nor the locals knew that there is a building called Nariman House with a synagogue in it at Colaba. The terrorists went for the Jews and they couldn't have done this without inside help".[28] At the Nariman House the NSG slithered down from helicopters on the top of the roof of the four floor building, in an extremely risky operation. The destruction here was by far the greatest with only a clam shell representing the old structure at the end of the operation.

One of the terrorist who had taken hostages called up a television channel, India TV from the cell phone of Rabbi Gavriel Noach Holtzberg and gave a number of grievances including the riots in Gujarat in 2002, demolition of the Babri Masjid in 1992 and the ongoing dispute over Kashmir. "Are you aware how many people have been killed in Kashmir? Are you aware how your army has killed Muslims? We die every day. It's better to win one day as a lion than die this way," said the terrorist as per records of transcripts of the conversation. Specific to the Chabad House hostages however his ire was against growing Indo Israeli ties. "You call their (Israeli) army staff to visit Kashmir. Who are they to come to J & K? This is a matter between us and the Hindus, the Hindu government. Why does Israel come here?" referring to reports of a recent visit of Israel's army chief, Maj. Gen. Avi Mizrahi, in September.[29] Rabi Taub's suspicions were thus proved right.

## The Bombs

The multiple components of the terror strike also included the proverbial weapon of the terrorists, bombs. The aim was obviously to create maximum confusion. There were ten bombs planted by the terrorists at various locations, two outside the Taj Hotel and Gokul restaurant, two in Oberoi Trident, two in the Taxis, one each inside the Taj, Nariman House, CST and BPCL Petrol Pump outside Nariman point. As per Mumbai police all were defused or exploded. Each had approximately 8 kgs of RDX. The delay switch of these bombs was programmable from 8 minutes 32 seconds to a maximum of 194 days.[30] The instructions for the timer were reported to be in Urdu. The timer was set for five hours indicating that the bombs were to go off during the critical period of evacuation of casualties.

The first bombs went off between 1030-1045 PM, blasts in two taxis at Vile Parle and another outside the Dockyard railway station.[31] "At Taj, the RDX bomb was kept in a small metal box inside a rucksack. The ball bearings in the bomb would act as shrapnel inflicting massive damage," an official said.[32] At the Trident, the RDX amount used is not known as it exploded before Bomb Disposal Squad officials could defuse it. Next to the entrance there was a huge dent following the blast and the window panes up to few metres were shattered. "We had spotted the bomb but since terrorists were firing continuously, we just covered it with a bomb blanket, reducing the impact of the explosion. It was quite scary," an official of the Mumbai police bomb squad said.[33]

At the CST the bomb was discovered much later. "The bags were found among abandoned luggage of persons who had been injured or killed in the attack on the night of November 26. The RDX was part of the five bombs planted by the terrorists. Searches are now being conducted on the (entire) station premises," Maria the Police officer heading the investigations in Mumbai said. Police said the bombs were spotted late because investigators misunderstood what Ajmal Amir Kasab, the lone terrorist arrested, told them during interrogation. "He had said they (the 10 terrorists) had planted five bombs. Three bombs were found last Thursday, two had been placed at the Taj and another near the Oberoi. It was thought that all (bombs) had been accounted for," Maria said. The other two bombs were initially thought to be those that went off in two taxis, one of them in Vile Parle. Maria believed that the taxi bombs were meant to kill the drivers so they wouldn't tell the police about the terrorists and, therefore, not part of the five planted in the city[34]

K.P. Raghuvanshi, the new chief of the Maharashtra anti-terror squad, said the timer devices failed to work despite being sophisticated because of faulty assembling. "Kasab has told us the bombs planted by the terrorists around Mumbai were assembled aboard hijacked trawler Kuber. The timing devices were like the ones commonly used by the Lashkar in Kashmir," he added. The pink packing material found in the Kuber was similar to that used to wrap the RDX bomb kept near the main entrance of the Taj, Raghuvanshi said, adding that the strings on the timers were also like those found on the trawler. [35]

**The Terrorists**

Based on the strikes and subsequent information collected by the investigators, it is presumed that there were two teams in Taj, one in Oberoi Trident and one in Nariman house. This accounts for eight terrorists. Two terrorists were accosted by the police at Girgaum Chowpatty, one of whom was killed and the second frequently referred to as Kasab is under the custody of the Mumbai police, thus making a total of ten terrorists.

The Mumbai commissioner of police Hasan Gafoor clarified a number of issues after the initial investigation setting aside many rumours floating in the media. For instance he stated that, "It is not true that they (terrorists) were familiar with the insides of the hotels." He also confirmed that there were only 10 terrorists, who had never come to Mumbai for a reconnaissance before and were a part of a suicide mission with no plans to return to Pakistan after the mission. The return route found on Global Positioning System (GPS) seized on Kuber fishing trawler was automatically generated by the programme rather than pre fed. As only one rubber dinghy was used it can be assumed that the figure given by the Police Commissioner is reasonable. These figures are confirmed based on recoveries made and tabulated as per Table[36&37].(Table at next page)

Each terrorist was armed with an AK 47 automatic rifle, a pistol, a Bomb, several grenades and hundreds of rounds of ammunition. Reports also indicate that they carried bags of dry fruit to sustain themselves in a long siege. It was a self contained team thus which could operate at will.

| Location | Recoveries | Likely Strength of Terrorists |
|----------|------------|-------------------------------|
| Nariman House | Two AK-47 rifles, nine magazines, two pistols and mobile phones | Two. Babar Imran alias Abu Akasha and Nasir alias Abu Umar. |
| Trident Oberoi | Two more AK-47 rifles, eight magazines and two pistols | Two. Abu Fahad alias Fahad Ullah and Chhota Abdul Rehman. |
| Taj | Four AK 47 rifles and allied equipment | Four. Hafiz Arshad alias Bada Abdul Rehman, Javed alias Abu Ali, Abu Shoaib, Nazir alias Abu Umed. |
| Girgaum Chowpatty | Two AK 47 rifles and allied equipment | Two. Abu Mujahid alias Ismail Khan and Mohammed Ajmal Amir alias Kasab. [38] |

## The Counter Terror Response

Let us visualize the counter terror response in detail. Remarking on the conduct of counter terror operations, the Indian Home Minister said in the parliament, "The operations were conducted under very difficult circumstances: the terrorists were heavily armed, there was a hostage situation, and the terrorists had the advantage of shield and height afforded by the tall buildings that they had entered. Nevertheless, through their patience, skill and bravery, the security forces were able to neutralise the terrorists and rescued hundreds of persons who had been trapped in the buildings. The operations came to an end at about 8.20 a.m. on November 29, 2008". [39]

Mumbai has seen violence before including gang warfare and bomb attacks. Thus the shooting was seen by many residents as another stand off between criminals and the police. It was only when the guns were targeted indiscriminately and there was automatic fire that perhaps the gravity of the situation was appreciated. Just then the bombs went off in two taxis, adding to the confusion. To the Mumbai police chief thus, the situation would have been certainly hazy, shootings at two places, bomb attacks at others and conflicting reports pouring in from all directions. The shoot outs including indiscriminate firing and bombs caught the police in Mumbai completely off guard for it was an unusual situation for police in any part of the World. This would be evident from the lack of interception of the group at the CST, where armed guards of the Railway Protection Force and the Mumbai police are deployed. As information about the terrorist attacks from the Nariman House, Taj Hotel and the Oberoi-Trident Hotel was received police parties were rushed to the places. The nature of the strike reveals that the terrorists were well armed and equipped but would have been easy to neutralize in the initial stages had the Mumbai police had a dedicated counter terror squad as the NSG fully equipped to deal with such a threat. After the terror attack many police forces in the country are planning to raise squads on the lines of the NSG for effective and timely response.

The police reaction to the terrorist attack generally came in three distinct phases comprising of the Mumbai police, the Marine Commandoes (MARCOS) and the National Security Guards (NSG) respectively. There was apparently no distinction between these three phases. The first phase was launched by the

Mumbai police which was an uncoordinated response by the Anti Terrorist Squad along with local police forces.

The Rapid Action Force of the CRPF which is primarily a riot control force reportedly took post to surround the locations where terrorists had taken hostages on the night of 26-27 November. Through out the night, small batches of guests at the hotel made their way out. In the second phase the Marine Commandos (MARCOS) started their clearance operation on 27 November in the Taj Mahal hotel awaiting the arrival of the NSG. Army snipers also took position around the buildings preventing escape.

Outlining the response of the Central government from Delhi, the Home Minister indicated in the Parliament, "Shortly before 11 p.m. on November 26, 2008, information was received by the Central Government that there were incidents of firing in several places in Mumbai. Immediately, the Central Government authorities got in touch with the authorities of the Government of Maharashtra. At the request of the Government of Maharashtra, the local Army and Navy authorities were asked to provide assistance. Accordingly, the Army deployed 5 columns to cordon off the affected areas and the Navy deployed their commandos to deal with the terrorists. Meanwhile, at about 11.30 p.m., the Government of Maharashtra asked for the National Security Guards. The Central Government immediately alerted the NSG and mobilized their counter terrorist units, based at Manesar in Haryana. A group of around 200 men (which was reinforced the next day) was airlifted to Mumbai late that night. They were deployed at the various sites of the operation in the early hours of November 27, 2008". [40]

In the third phase thus the National Security Guards launched Operation Cyclone with the aim of relieving the hostages in Taj, Oberoi Trident and Nariman House, on 27 November. In 24 hours of operations the NSG cleared the Oberoi by 3 PM on 28 November and the Nariman House the same night. The Taj hotel was last to be cleared at 9 AM on 29 November. [41] "All operations are over. The NSG has formally reported that the operations are complete and now Taj, Oberoi and Nariman House are being sanitised. There are no more terrorists now in Mumbai. All have been liquidated or captured alive," M L Kumawat, Special Secretary in the Union Home Ministry told reporters in Delhi on 29 November 2008.

While two NSG personnel were killed in the operations, eight commandos were injured. The authorities refused to negotiate with terrorists unlike in the past in which in high profile cases as kidnapping of the daughter of then Home Minister Mr Mufti Mohammad Sayeed or the hijacking of the IC 814. [42]

Simultaneously the Coast Guard and the Indian Navy launched extensive maritime reconnaissance and surveillance operations in the Arabian Sea with 20 Navy and Coast Guard ships spread out for area patrolling of the region from bases at Mumbai, Goa, Daman, Porbunder, Jakhau and Okha. [43] The government also asked the Navy and Coast Guard to scan the 1,200-odd uninhabited islands in the maritime zone.

In a report on 1 December Health Department of the Maharashtra government confirmed that 172 people were killed in the terror attacks, 248 admitted in the hospitals and 44 were taking treatment in outpatient department.[44] 26 foreign nationals lost their lives while 22 were injured.[45] Those killed included three Germans, two Canadians and six Israelis, one American, Briton, Thai, Japanese, Australian, Italian and Chinese each and three unknown persons. Mr. E. Ahamed, Minister of State for External Affairs at the UN Security Council on Threats to International Peace and Security Caused by Terrorist Acts gave the casualty figures as, "179 persons, including 26 foreigners".[46] The Home Minister in a statement to the Indian Parliament on 11 December 2008 however indicated that 164 persons (civilians and security personnel) including 26 foreigners lost their lives and 308 persons were injured. Besides, nine terrorists were killed by security forces in the operations.[47] As a follow up the police registered cases and investigations are under progress by the Crime Branch of the Mumbai Police with support from the Maharashtra Police and the Central agencies. [48]

## The Relief Operations

The nature of the strike entailed not just rescue of hostages and evacuation of casualties but also relief to the large number of people particularly the foreigners stranded in Mumbai. Hundreds of people were rescued from the two hotels, amongst the VIPs rescued was Member of Parliament Jaisingrao Gaikwad holed up at the Taj Hotel, who survived on apples and water for two days. The Embassies in New Delhi went fully operational to provide relief to citizens entrapped in the hotels. A Control Room (CR) was also established by the Ministry of External Affairs to assist Indian and Foreign Missions. The CR was manned round – the – clock with multiple numbers and a separate fax facility.

Consulates of countries in the City were active providing all the help required to the rescued hostages and the escapees. The British had located the Deputy High Commissioner there, Vicki Teadall who set up a special centre for assistance. She was reported by the Times of India as saying," We are ensuring they get empathy and help, food and drink and hotel bookings before sending them back home".[49] Similar arrangements were made by the Australian High commission with additional staff being despatched from Delhi.

## Ajmal's Statement, According to Police

The following is a statement attributed by Mumbai police sources to Mohammed Ajmal Amir Iman alias Abu Mujahid, the lone gunman captured alive during the Mumbai attacks. The statement was recorded while the attacks were on and it is possible that the suspect has changed his version during subsequent rounds of interrogation. The statement, including spelling, is being reproduced verbatim.[50]

Age: 21 yrs.

Occupation: Labor, R/ — Faridkot, Tehsil — Dipalpur, Dist — Ukada

State: Suba Punjab, Pakistan

I am as above and reside at the above given address since my birth. I have studied up to 4th standard from Government Primary School. After leaving school in 2000, I went to Lahore. My brother Afzal stays at galli No. 54, R.No. 12, Mohalla — Tohit Abad, near Yadgar Minar, Lahore. I did labor jobs at different places till 2005. During that period I used to visit my native place.

In the year 2005, I had quarrel with my father. Therefore, I left my house and went to Ali Hajveri Darbar at Lahore. At the said place, the boys who had run away from their houses are kept. From there, the boys are sent to different places for employment.

One day when I was there, a person by name Shafiq came there and took me with him. He was in the catering business. He was from Zhelam. I started working with him on daily wages. I was given Rs 120 per day. After some days my salary was increased up to Rs 200 per day. I worked with him till 2007.

While I was working with Shafiq, I came in contact with one Muzaffar Lal Khan, aged 22 years, r/ — Village — Romiya, Tehsil & Dist — Atak, State — Sarhad, Pakistan. As we were not getting enough money, we decided to carry out Robbery/dacoity at some place so that we will get a large amount. As such we left the job.

Thereafter we went to Rawalpindi. We hired a flat at Bangash Colony, Rawalpindi, and started residing in it. Afzal had located a house where he thought we would get a large amount. He had surveyed the said place and drawn a map of the said place. We required some fire-arms for our purpose. Afzal told me that, he could get some fire-arms at his native place but it was very risky as there was frequent checking at his native place.

While we were in search of fire-arms we saw some L-e-T stalls at Raja bazaar, Rawalpindi, on the day of Bakri-id. We thought that, even if we procured fire-arms, we could not operate them. Therefore, we decided to join L-e-T for weapon training. After making enquiries we reached L-e-T office. In the L-e-T office we met a person. We told him that, we wanted to join L-e-T. He made some enquiry with us, noted our names and address and told us to come on next day.

On the next day we went to L-e-T office and met the same man. One more person was present with him. He gave us Rs 200

and some receipt. Then he gave us the address of a place called
Marqas Taiyyaba, Muridke, and told us to go to the said place
where L-e-T is having their training camp.

As directed we went to the said place by bus. We showed
the receipt given to us at the gate of the camp. We were allowed
inside. At the entry gate our details were filled up on two forms.
Then we were taken to the actual camp area.

At the said place, initially we were selected for 21 days
training called Daura-Sufa. From the next day, we started
attending training. The daily program was as mentioned below.

04.15           - Wake up call and thereafter namaz
08.00           - Breakfast
08.30-10.00     - Lecture on Hadis and Quran by Mufti Sayyed
10.00-12.00     - Rest
12.00-13.00     - Lunch Break
13.00-14.00     - Namaz
14.00-16.00     - Rest
16.00-18.00     - P.T. and Game Instructor — Fadulla
18.00-20.00     - Namaz and other work
20.00-21.00     - Dinner

After completion of the above said training, we were
selected for another training called Daura-Ama. The said training
was also for 21 days. We were then taken in a vehicle to a place
called Mansera, Buttal Village. At the said place we were given
training of all weapons for 21 days.

The daily program was as mentioned below.

| | |
|---|---|
| 04.15 - 05.00 | - Wake up call and thereafter namaz |
| 05.00-06.00 | - P.T. Instructor — Abu Anas |
| 08.00 | - Breakfast |
| 08.30-11.30 | - Weapons training. — Trainer — Abdul Rehman, |
| Weapons | - AK-47, Green-, SKS, Uzi gun, pistol, revolver |
| 11.30-12.00 | - Rest |
| 12.00-13.00 | - Lunch break |
| 13.00-14.00 | - Namaz |
| 14.00-16.00 | - Rest |
| 16.00-18.00 | - P.T. |
| 18.00-20.00 | - Namaz and other work |
| 20.00-21.00 | - Dinner |

After completing the said training, we were told that, we will be given the next advance training but for that purpose we have to do some Khidmat for two months (Khidmat is a sort of service in the said camp as per the trainees liking). We agreed to do the Khidmat for two months. After two months I was allowed to go to meet my parents. I stayed with my parents for one month. Thereafter, I went to L-e-T camp situated at Shaiwainala, Muzzafarabad for further advanced training. At that place they took my photographs and filled up some forms. Then we were taken to Chelabandi pahadi area for training called Duara-khas. The said training was for 3 months.

The training included P.T., handling of all weapons and firing practice of the said weapons, training of handling of Hand grenade, rocket launchers and mortars.

The daily program was as mentioned below.

04.15-05.00        — Wake up call and thereafter namaz

05.00-06.00        — P.T. Instructor Abu Mawiya

08.00              — Breakfast

08.30-11.30        — Weapons training handling of all weapons and firing practices of the said weapons, training of handling of hand grenade, rocket launchers and mortars, Green-, SKS, Uzi gun, pistol, revolver, Hand grenade, rocket launchers. Trainer — Abu Mawiya

11.30-12.00        — Rest

12.00-13.00        — Lunch Break

13.00-14.00        — Namaz

14.00-16.00        — Weapon training and firing practice. Lecture on Indian security agencies

16.00-18.00        — P.T.

18.00-20.00        — Namaz and other work

20.00-21.00        — Dinner

At the said place 32 persons were present for training. Out of these 32 trainees, 16 were selected for some confidential operation by one Zaqi-ur-Rehman Chacha. Out of these 16 trainees 3 trainees ran away from the camp. The above said chacha then sent the remaining 13 of us along with a person called Kafa to the above said earlier camp at Muridke. At Muridke we were taught swimming and getting acquainted with the environment experienced by a fisherman on a sea. We did some experimental tours by launches on the sea. During the said training we were given lectures on working of Indian security agencies. We were shown the clippings highlighting the atrocities on Muslims in India.

After completing the said training we were allowed to go to our native places. For seven days I stayed with my family members. After seven days I went to the L-e-T camp at Muzzafarabad. The above said 13 of us were present for training. Thereafter as per the instructions of Zaki-ur-Rehman, the above said kafa took us to camp at Muridke.

At the said camp again we underwent the training of swimming and getting acquainted with the environment and experience on sea. The training continued for one month. During the said training we were given the lectures on India and its security agencies including RAW. We were also given the training on how to evade the chase by security personnel. We were strictly instructed not to make phone calls to Pakistan after reaching India. The names of the persons present for the said training are as mentioned below.

1) Mohd Azmal @ Abu Muzahid
2) Ismail @ Abu Umar
3) Abu Ali
4) Abu Aksha
5) Abu Umer
6) Abu Shoeb
7) Abdul Rehman (Bada)
8) Abdul Rehaman (Chota)
9) Afadulla
10) Abu Umar

After completion of training, Zaki-ur-Rehaman @ chacha selected 10 of us and formed 5 teams each having two persons on

15 Sept 2008. My team included myself and Ismail. Our code name was VTS team. We were then shown the site 'google earth' on internet. On the same site we were shown the information about Azad Maidan, Mumbai, how and where to get down at Mumbai. We were shown the film on VT railway station and the film showing the commuters moving around at rush hours at VT railway station.

We were instructed to carry out the firing at rush hours in the morning between 7 to 11 hours and between 7 to 11 hours in the evening. Then kidnap some persons, take them to the roof of some nearby building. After reaching at the roof top, we were to contact chacha. After that, chacha would give the telephone or mobile no of electronic media. We were then to contact the media persons on the same phone.

And as per the instructions received from Chacha, we would make demands for releasing the hostages. This was the general strategy decided by our trainers. The date fixed for the said operation was 27th Sept 2008. However, the operation was cancelled for some reason. We stayed at Karachi. Again we made practice of travelling by speed boats on the sea. We stayed there upto 23rd nov 2008. The other teams were as mentioned below.

2nd Team
1) Abu Aksha
2) Abu Umar
3rd Team
1) Bada Abdul Rehman
2) Abu Ali

4th Team

1) Chhota Abdul Rehman

2) Afadulla

5th Team

1) Shoeb

2) Abu Umer

On 23rd Nov 2008 the above said teams including our team left from Azizabad, Karachi along with Zaki-ur-Rehman @ Chacha and Kafa. We were taken to the nearby sea shore. At 04.15 hours we reached the sea shore. At the sea shore we boarded a launch. After travelling for 22 to 25 nautical miles we met a bigger launch in the sea. We boarded the said launch and after journey of 1 hour we boarded a bigger ship by name Al-Huseini in the deep sea.

While boarding the said ship each of us was given a sack containing 8 grenades, one A.K. 47 rifle, 200 cartridges, 2 magazines and one cell phone for communication. Then we started towards Indian coast. When we reached Indian waters, the crew members of Al-Huseini ship hijacked one Indian launch. The seamen from the said launch were shifted to Al-Huseini ship. We were then boarded the hijacked Indian ship. One Indian seaman was kept along with us. At the gun point he took us towards the Indian coast. After journey of about 3 days, we reached near sea shore of Mumbai. While we were at some distance from the shore, Ismail and Afadulla killed the Indian seaman, (Tandel) at the basement of the said Indian launch. Then we boarded flatable Dinghi and reached Budwar Park Jetty as per the instructions received earlier.

After getting down at Budwar Park I went along with Ismail to V.T. railway Stn by taxi. After reaching the hall of V.T. railway stn. we, i.e. Ismail and myself went to the common toilet, took out the weapons from our sacks, loaded them, came out of toilet and started firing indiscriminately towards the passengers. Suddenly one police officer in uniform came towards us and opened fire. In retaliation we threw hand grenades towards him and also opened fire towards him. Then we went inside the railway stn threatening the commuters and randomly firing at them. Then we came out of the railway stn. and started searching for a building with roof top. But we did not find a suitable building. Therefore we entered a lane. Then we entered a building and went upstarts.

On 3rd or 4th floor we searched for hostages but we found that the said building was a hospital and not a residential building. Therefore we started coming down. At that time policemen started firing at us. As such we threw some grenades towards them. When we were coming out of the hospital premises, we suddenly saw one police vehicle passing in front of us. Therefore we took shelter behind a bush.

Another vehicle passed in front of us and stopped at some distance. One police officer got down from the said vehicle and started firing at us. One bullet hit my hand and my AK 47 dropped down. I bent to pick it up when second bullet hit me on the same hand. I got injured. Ismail opened fire at the officers who were in said vehicle. They got injured and firing from their side stopped.

We waited for some time and then went towards the said the said vehicle. Three bodies lying there. Ismail removed the three bodies and drove the said vehicle. I sat next to him. While we were moving in the said vehicle, some police men tried to stop us. Ismail opened fire towards them while we were on the move; our vehicle got punctured near a big ground by the side of road.

Ismail got down from the driver seat, stopped a car at the gun point and removed the three lady occupants from the said car. Then Ismail carried me to the car and sat me inside as I was injured. Then he drove the said car.

While we were moving in the said car, we were stopped on the road near sea shore. Ismail fired towards them. Some policemen got injured. Police also opened fire towards us. Due to the police firing Ismail got injured. Then police removed us to some hospital. In the hospital I came to know that Ismail succumbed to the injuries, he has sustained.

My statement is read over to me explained in Hindi and it is correctly recorded.

---

**(Endnotes)**

1 HM announces measures to enhance security. Available at http:// pib.nic.in/release/release.asp?relid=45446&kwd=.

2 Coast Guard locates suspected terrorist ship M V Alpha. Times of India Report 27 November 2008. Available at http:// t i m e s o f i n d i a . i n d i a t i m e s . c o m /

Coast_Guard_locates_suspected_terrorist_ship_M_V_Alpha/
articleshow/3765920.cms

3 Coordinated attacks in Mumbai: Chronology. Zee News Report. Available at http://www.zeenews.com/Nation/2008-11-27/ 486793news.html

4 HM announces measures to enhance security. Available at http:// pib.nic.in/release/release.asp?relid=45446&kwd=

5 Admiralty Manual of Seamanship: 1995 Edition. Hmst, Great Britain Ministry of Defence. London. Accessed on Google books 5-8.

6 Hijacked ship with sat phone seized. Times of India 28 November 2008. New Delhi. P 10.

7 The Anatomy of Terror. The Times of India. 30 November 2008. p 12

8 Chhatrapati Shivaji Terminus. Available at Chhatrapati Shivaji Terminus (CST).

9 Coordinated attacks in Mumbai: Chronology. Zee News Report. Available at http://www.zeenews.com/Nation/2008-11-27/ 486793news.html.

10 The Anatomy of Terror. The Times of India. 30 November 2008. p 12

11 Times of India Report. LeT Did It : Arrested Gunman. Times of India 28 November 2008. p 10.

12 HM announces measures to enhance security. Available at http:// pib.nic.in/release/release.asp?relid=45446&kwd=.

13 Sagnik Chaudhury. Killing spree from CST to Chowpatty claimed top cops. Indian Express. 29 November 2008. New Delhi. P 4.

14 Regina Anthony Nair. Attacks a setback for tourism, hospitality biz. The Mint. 28 November 2008. New Delhi. P 4.

15 The Anatomy of Terror. The Times of India. 30 November 2008. p 12.

16 2 gunmen in Taj Hotel, 7 foreigners among 15 hostages. PTI Report. Available at http://ibnlive.in.com/news/2-gunmen-in-taj-hotel-7-foreigners-among-15-hostages/79132-3.html

17 Ritu Sarin. Hotel jala do. Sunday Express. 30 November 2008. New Delhi. P 1-2.

18 Swatee Kher. Sandeep died trying to save me: NSG Commando. Sunday Express. 30 November 2008. New Delhi. P 9.

19 Ritu Sarin. Taj sanitized, its helpful staff back to work. Sunday Express. 30 November 2008. New Delhi. P 1.

20 Regina Anthony Nair. Attacks a setback for tourism, hospitality biz. The Mint. 28 November 2008. New Delhi. P 4.

21 Trident Mumbai. Available at http://www.tridenthotels.com/mumbai_nariman_point/index.asp

22 Times of India Report. Snipers in position near Nariman House. Times of India 28 November 2008. p 10.

23 Emily Wax. Calls Shed Light on Gunmen's Motives. Available at http://www.washingtonpost.com/wp-dyn/content/article/2008/12/15/AR2008121502717_pf.html

24 Upneet Pansare. The horrors within. Sunday Express. 30 November 2008. New Delhi. P 18.

25 Ritu Sarin. We had to move in a slow, calibrated manner. The Indian Express. 28 November 2008. New Delhi. P 5.

26 Shweta Desai. Nariman House now a charred shell. Sunday Express. 30 November 2008. New Delhi. P 18.

27 Mohan Kumar. Rabbi's body found with legs tied. Sunday Express. 30 November 2008. New Delhi. P 18.

28 Shalini Naik. Israeli's trapped even in death. Sunday Express. 30 November 2008. New Delhi. P 16.

29 Emily Wax. Calls Shed Light on Gunmen's Motives. Available at http://www.washingtonpost.com/wp-dyn/content/article/2008/12/15/AR2008121502717_pf.html

30 C Unnikrishnan.3 RDX bombs found around Taj and Trident, TNN Repoιʀ. Available at http://economictimes.indiatimes.com/articleshow/3777750.cms

31 Indian Express Report. From the Landing to the Attack. The Indian Express. 3 December 2008. New Delhi. P 9.

32 3 RDX bombs found around Taj and Trident

http://timesofindia.indiatimes.com/India/3_RDX_bombs_found_around_Taj_and_Trident/articleshow/3777638.cms

33 3 RDX bombs found around Taj and Trident

http://timesofindia.indiatimes.com/India/3_RDX_bombs_found_around_Taj_and_Trident/articleshow/3777638.cms

34. Bags of bomb in wounded Mumbai station

Daily Telegraph Report 4 December 2008.

35 Bags of bomb in wounded Mumbai station

Daily Telegraph Report 4 December 2008

36 Battle for Mumbai ends, death toll rises to 195. Available at http://timesofindia.indiatimes.com/articleshow/msid-3771119,flstry-1.cms

37. 59-hour siege of old Taj hotel ends; 4 holed up Terrorists killed. Available at http://72.14.235.132/search?q=cache:OuDDgeF6XVEJ:www.ddinews.gov.in/DDNews/Templates/NewsDetail.aspx%3FNRMODE%3DPublished%26NRORIGINALURL%3D%252FHomepage%252FHomepage%252520%252520Top%252520Story%252Ftrf.htm%26NRNODEGUID%3D%257B7A83BA2A-EBBE-4761-AAC9-E27E0A1C88A3%257D%26NRCACHEHINT%3DNoModifyGuest +No+RDX +was +found +by+commandos+but+they+recovered+grenades,+AK-

47+rifles,+pistols+and+mobile+phones.&hl=en&ct=clnk&cd=3&gl=uk

38 Faces of Mumbai's 26/11 Terror. Times Of India. 10 December 2008. New Delhi. P 11.

39 HM announces measures to enhance security. Available at http:// pib.nic.in/release/release.asp?relid=45446&kwd=.

40 Ibid.

41 Indian Express Report. The Siege and the Rescue. The Indian Express. 4 December 2008. New Delhi. P 9.

42 Times of India Report. In a first, India refuses to negotiate with terrorists. Times of India 28 November 2008. p 7.

43 Navy, Coast Guard step up patrolling along high seas. Available at http://economictimes.indiatimes.com/articleshow/3783758.cms

44 Rahi Gaikwad. Terror Attack death Toll 172: Health Department. The Hindu. 1 December 2008. new Delhi p 11.

45 Rahi Gaikwad. Terror Attack death Toll 172: Health Department. The Hindu. 1 December 2008. new Delhi p 11

46 Mr. E. Ahamed, Minister of State for External Affairs at the UN Security Council on Threats to International Peace and Security Caused by Terrorist Acts. MEA India Press Release 9 December 2008. Available at www.meaindia.nic.in

47 HM announces measures to enhance security. Available at http:// pib.nic.in/release/release.asp?relid=45446&kwd=

48 Ibid.

49 Consulates Work overtime to sent citizens home to safety. Times of India Report. Times of India. 29 November 2008. New Delhi. P 10.

50 Ajmal's statement, according to police: Daily Telegraph 12 December 2008. Available at http://www.telegraphindia.com/ 1081211/jsp/nation/story_10236283.jsp

# 3

## Mumbaikar Strikes Back

*"The citizens have come together to keep Mumbai a city that is peaceful and united and to build a world based on the principles of tolerance and peace, equality and justice."*

Activist Jatin Desai

Mumbai, the melting pot of all cultures Indian from the Parsi to the Bhaiyya from Uttar Pradesh, the Anna from Chennai to the Ghati from Ratnagiri in Maharashtra is known for its resilience. The city has been the target of many terror attacks before as is shown in Appendix B below. In 1993, Mumbai saw extensive riots as a backlash to the serial bombings attributed to Dawood Ibrahim, a notorious gang warlord now allegedly living in Karachi, Pakistan. In July 1986, in serial bombings in local trains, life line of Mumbai commuters, 187 people lost their lives. The images of Mumbai's citizens known as, "Mumbaikars (Mumbai person)" an asexual epithet carrying the injured in a show of solidarity across railways tracks remains etched in the minds of many.

26/11 was a little different, Mumbaikars took some what longer to recover, but they made a triumphant come back none the less. Whether it was the 41$^{st}$ century in Test cricket by

Mumbai's little master Sachin Tendulkar or opening of Café Leopold three days after the attack, the maximum city showed that it would not be cowed down by dastardly terror. Amongst the unlikeliest of heroes was the announcer at the CST Railway station, Mr V D Zende. Perched from a vantage point, he saw the mayhem but did not panic and instead guided a large number of people away from the site of firing from Platform No 1. By the time the terrorists had reached this point, it was deserted. Then there were the brave policemen, the Salaskars and Ongoles, who went into encounters knowing fully well that they were facing a new challenge. Yet they did not dither.

One thing though was different this time. The citizens of Mumbai demanded that heads roll and the politically insensitive local leaders as the Chief Minister who was seen taking his actor son along with a well known film director around the scene of the incident the very next day all clear was given had to leave. The naiveté of the father-son duo was astonishing for they failed to appreciate that the public would not be so gullible as to disassociate the presence of the film director from a proposed movie on the ghastly tragedy, even before blood had been wiped off the floors of the hotel. The State Home Minister who attempted to play down the incident as some thing which was normal in large cities also had to leave. His counter part in the Centre had become a mill stone around the leadership of his party had preceded him. This was the citizen's retribution over an insensitive and incompetent leadership. Mumbai's corporates were hit the hardest for many noted bankers, developers and lawyers were lost in the strike, Ashok Kapur, non executive chairman of Yes Bank, developer Pankaj Shah and solicitor Anand

Bhatt amongst others were a loss to the city.[1] The Prime Minister Mr Manmohan Singh and the new Home Minister Mr P Chidambaram sensing the mood were quick to apologise to the nation.

But the protests were peaceful with formation of human chains at the spots targeted by terrorists and other key areas to condemn the terror attacks. The tone was for peace and not violence. "We have seen so much of hatred and bloodshed in our city that we will not give in to terror and to those who preach war, violence, hatred and intolerance," activist Jatin Desai said. The long chains running across the island city extended to the eastern and western suburbs.[2]

The response was overwhelming as a chain started from Nariman House to Oberoi Trident Hotels, via 4th Pasta Lane, Free Press Road and NCPA. While a second route covered the west side of Oberoi Trident Hotels to S V Road, via Metro Junction, Kemps Corner, Worli Naka and Mahim causeway. A third route was from Nariman House to S V Road, via Hutatma Chowk, CST, Crawford Market, Byculla Flyover, Dadar TT, Sion Circle, and Mahim causeway. They were people of all religions and creed who came together for the common cause of solidarity after the great tragedy. It gave them confidence to survive the vestiges of terror, which had caused a temporary psychological impact on the mind.[3]

The real Mumbai, the spirit of the city, which knows no caste, creed, language or religion, where Keralite, Punjabi, Bihar, Gujarati and Marathi all become one, moved on. The remarkable resilience of Mumbai was evident with Leopold Café, known as Leo, for many was up for breakfast on 30 November three days after the terrorists fired indiscriminately. The owner Jehani said emphatically to the Sunday Express, "We didn't close even during the riots. So my primary concern is to reopen. Mumbai believes in looking ahead. Nothing can dent its spirit". Opened first in 1871 and converted from an oil store, it maintains its distinctive touch. In 1987 it acquired three foot beer towers unique for a city pub.[4] Scrubbed clean before the reopening, images of loyal customers back in Leopold were on the television screens beaming possibly the first positive pictures after the attack.

The Taj and the Trident large properties extended over several floors and carpet area took a little longer to reopen. On Sunday, 21 December even a month before the great tragedy, both Taj and Trident had opened. "She has stood for more than a 100 years and will stand for a 100 more. It was a challenge to have the hotel reopen in some form within a month of the attack. We may have been knocked down but will never be knocked out," said Tata Group Chairman Ratan Tata at the reopening. The guests were all there on an occasion filled with emotion as the 550 employees of the Hotel marched into the lobby of the Tower wing to the applause of the waiting crowd of the city's top industrialists, bureaucrats and socialites. Karambir Kang was no doubt the hero of the day. The general manager had lost his wife and two children in the attack but Kang had rescued many lives and now he was in the fore front in renovation of the hotel. It was truly a mission fulfilled for this great human being.

The foreign travelers and regular businessmen stood behind the Mumbaikar. . "If you travel a lot, you just get caught up in things sometimes," said Mike Potter, from England. "I've traveled lots of places and with a healthy dose of common sense have avoided any major problems. But then again, I was in Leopold's a couple days ago, and who knows what could have happened had the timing been different, through no fault of my own." Foreigners in other cities in India were also not deterred. "It could happen anywhere," said a Finnish tourist who was shopping at Connaught Place in New Delhi. "It's just bad luck if you are in that place when it happens. It could happen in my hometown." "I don't feel nervous about being here," said a Swedish woman at Khan Market, New Delhi who had arrived a week ago on vacation. "There are crazy people everywhere."[5] The infectious sanguine spirit of Mumbai had affected these men and women from far away land.

Behind Mumbai was the media, conveying the atmosphere of gloom from 26 to 29 November, of somber remembrance thereafter followed by cynical hatred of the political class and finally the return of the spirit of the city, it encapsulated all. As the events happened in a premier metro, new media and television reporting came into its own. While the latter came up for harsh criticism from various quarters for its imbalanced reporting obviously due to lack of experience of covering such incidents, bloggers were seen to carry the day with responsible, public spirited messages seeking blood donations, providing information about relatives and friends and so on. For many bloggers as Arzan who posted on Mumbaimetblogs it was a first experience of, "live blogging during a bombing/hostage situation".[6]

There were many glitches as well. Lack of regulation and understanding of where the medium can reach in such a situation had resulted in the NSG's movement from Delhi to Mumbai being declared by the Home Minister on television and channels showing ticker headlines with 800 army·soldiers in operations were to create a flutter in media as well as security circles.[7]

The absence of any regulation during the event was evident with the television cameras panning on endlessly into terror sites and news anchors blaring operational details something which as per the BBC would have never been permitted in the West.[8] At the same time media commentators as Saubhik Chakrabarti remarked about the energy displayed by the news channels which kept the masses fairly well informed about the happenings at the sites.[9]

Nalin Mehta author of, "India on Television" writing on television coverage of the Mumbai attack in the Indian Express states, "channels are more numerous, competition far more intense and most importantly the attack on Mumbai is part of an entirely different canvas".[10] Calling the Indian electronic media surge as an, "industry infamous for its sensationalism", Mehta seeks better training and sensitisation of reporters and gain specialisation in reporting terrorist incidents given the frequency with which this is happening in the country. This would be away from the normal security beat which comprises of standard reporting on happenings in the field of defence and security. It is also something beyond crime reporting to which most reporters are more attuned.

The Mumbai terror strikes were headlined across international media, indicating that India had arrived on the global terrorism scene. The type and intensity of attacks, involvement of a large number of foreigners and initial reports that the terrorists were seeking victims with Western passports brought the interest to a high pitch, thereby resulting in extensive coverage of the incident across the globe.

Many lost their lives in Mumbai, but the spirit of the brave hearts of India's commercial capital including the relatives of those who died denoted the inner resilience and resolve of the masses. Mumbai the maximum city not just survived but was stronger, yet it was a sad reminder of the vulnerability of the metro. Hopefully the Mumbaikars courage need not be tested another time.

**Appendix B**

## Terror Attacks in Mumbai

Four major terrorist attacks have occurred in India's financial capital Mumbai in the last 15 years as per chronology given below:-

- Nov 26 - 29, 2008: 172 killed and hundreds injured in terror attacks in South Mumbai.

- July 11, 2006: 187 killed in seven blasts on suburban trains and stations.

- Aug 25, 2003: 46 people killed in two blasts including one near the Gateway of India.

- March 12, 1993: A series of bomb blasts left 257 dead and around 700 injured. Buildings attacked included the Bombay Stock Exchange, hotels, theatres, passport office, Air India building and Sahar Airport.[11]

## (Endnotes)

1 Mumbai Loses Some of its Best and Brightest. Times of India Report. Times of India. 29 November 2008. New Delhi. P 1.

2 Mumbai citizens form human chain to protest terror attacks. Press Trust of India Report. http://origin.ndtv.com/convergence/ndtv/ mumbaiterrorstrike/Story.aspx?ID=NEWEN20080076209&type=News

3 Ibid.

4 Alaka Sahani. Welcome back, Leo's up for breakfast today. Sunday Express. 30 November 2008. New Delhi. P 1-2.

5 Jessica Thompson. Foreigners unfazed in Delhi after Mumbai attacks. Available at

http://timesofindia.indiatimes.com/Cities/ Foreigners_unfazed_in_Delhi/articleshow/3780317.cms

6 Anubhuti Vishnoi. I don't care if this post does not make sense. Indian Express. 29 November 2008. New Delhi. P 5.

7 Manu Pubby and Anubhuti Vishnoi. Patil goof up, TV cameras 'compromise'. Indian Express. 28 November 2008. New Delhi. P 5.

8 Saubhik Chakravarty. Breaking Down News. Indian Express. 29 November 2008. New Delhi. P 13.

9 Saubhik Chakravarty. Breaking Down News. Indian Express. 29 November 2008. New Delhi. P 13.

10 Nalin Mehta. Eyes on Terror. Indian Express. 29 November 2008. New Delhi. P 12.

11 With inputs from Zee news Report. Major terror attacks in Mumbai: Timeline. Available at http://www.zeenews.com/nation/2008-11-27/ 486885news.html

# 4

# Tracing the Terrorist Group
## The LeT

*"The equipment, training and sophistication of their planning would tend to indicate a Pakistani link."*

Mr K Subrahmanyam

### Homing on to the Lashkar E Taiyyaba

Even as the counter terror operations were going on in South Mumbai, intelligence officials were homing on to the terrorist group responsible for the strike. The level and sophistication of the attack narrowed down the likely organisation to a group with a Pakistani connection. The Lashkar-e-Toiba (LeT) and Jaish-e-Mohammad were the two organizations suspected initially. These have resources to impart rigorous training to young men, and command them to kill themselves. Preliminary investigations also revealed links to the Lashkar e Taiyyaba (LeT) based on intercepts of conversations of the terrorists to Yusuf Muzammil, Muzaffarabad chief of LeT operations and an individual identified as Yahya in Bangladesh who is reported to have arranged SIM cards for the cell phones and fake identity cards from countries like Mauritius, UK, US and Australia. Calls were also traced to Zakir Ur Rehman, chief of training of the LeT and from the satellite phones on the MV Kuber to Jalalabad in

Pakistan.[1] Zaki-ur-Rehman Lakhvi, the Lashkar-e-Taiba 'commander', was reportedly based in Karachi for the last three months planning and coordinating the operation. Even Pakistani commentators talked of a Lashkar possibility at least in terms of capability. "The Lashkar definitely has the capability and the capacity to conduct attacks such as those which took place in Mumbai," said Rasool Baksh Raees, a political science professor at the Lahore University of Management Sciences.[2] Interrogation of the apprehended terrorist, Ajmal Amir confirmed the affiliation of the terrorists to the Lashkar e Taiyyaba.

An analysis of Email carried out by experts supported the premise that Lashkar e Taiyyaba was behind the attack says Praveen Swami in a report in the Hindu of 1 December. The use of the phrase Hyderabad Deccan is seen as a typical Pakistani connotation to differentiate from the city of the same name in Pakistan and is never used in India. The Lashkar claims made in various speeches such as the Convention in February 2000 has stated the aim is to terminate Indian rule in Hyderabad and Junagadh. The mail also uses, "Baniya" the word for trader in Hindi in derogative terms which is commonly used in Lashkar invectives from time to time.[3]

Further investigations including interrogation of the terrorist apprehended revealed that the Lashkar-e-Taiba commanders had ordered execution of a major fidayeen attack in Mumbai. In a conference in Muridke in Pakistan held under the aegis of its mother organization the Jamaat-ud-Dawa (JuD) as the Lashkar is banned in Pakistan, JuD chief Hafiz Saeed is said to have sought punishment on India for its activities in Afghanistan.[4]

Way back in November 1999, Hafiz Muhammad Sa'eed declared, "Today I announce the break-up of India, *Inshallah*. We will not rest until the whole of India is dissolved into Pakistan".[5] While Amir Hamza, senior Markaz official and editor of its Urdu organ, *ad-Da'wa*, thundered: "We ought to disintegrate India and even wipe India out".[6] Thus Lashkar activists have been apprehended in far away locations in the hinterland including Bangalore, Mysore, and Hyderabad and even near Tirupati, where one of the holiest Hindu shrines is located. The Lashkar-i-Taiba's motivations for an attack at Mumbai are many. It has a list of grievances against India which goes back to the 17th century to the Partition of the Sub Continent in 1947, and stretches to growing ties between India and the US as well as Israel.[7]

Praveen Swami based on interviews with key officers involved in the interrogation of the sole terrorist apprehended indicates that the group of 10 had been trained for months in marine combat and navigation skills, shown the maps of south Mumbai and films of targets tasked to hit. The prominent Lashkar leaders who were part of the attack plan were confirmed as Zakiur-Rahman Lakhvi alias Chachu, Zarrar Shah and Muzammil.

The captured terrorist was named by many sources in the press as Kamaal and Kasav, but Swami was the first to identify him as Mohammad Ajmal Amir Iman tasked to target the CST. The original plan was to leave for Mumbai on 27 September but was later delayed to 22 November.[8] Iman belonging to a poor family of Faridkot in Pakistan was provided, "Daura Aam" or normal training and "Daura Khas" advanced training by the

Lashkar and later specialized marine and navigation training once he was assigned to the suicide attack unit identified to target Mumbai. He was promised that his family which had rejected him when he was unemployed but showed much respect when he returned home on vacation during the training period would be given Rs 1.5 lakh by the Lashkar military commander.[9]

In a report in the Hindu, an Observer story which had traced Ajmal Amir, "kasab" to his village in Faridkot Pakistan was also published. The Observer has given the voter identity card numbers of parents of Amir and also confirmed his parentage through records. Kasab's father is Mohammad Amir Iman and mother Noor Elahi. They are both registered voters with national identity card numbers 3530121767339 and 3530157035058 respectively said the report.[10]

The suave disinformation campaign by the LeT indicates sophistication in an organization which preaches fundamentalism. The LeT cleverly propped up a decoy organisation the Deccan Mujahideen which claimed responsibility. The Deccan Mujahideen was also useful in that it could be related to India. To divert the trail, the LeT's Kashmir arm also refuted allegations that the attack was made by the organisation. Immediately after the strikes, the JuD also launched a media offensive against accusations of its involvement taking a team around its complex in Muridke escorted by Abdullah Muntazir, a spokesman. "All the allegations against us are baseless," Abdullah said and condemned the Mumbai attacks as "un-Islamic". He pointed that since the organization spoke against

India, each time an attack takes place,. "So they are making propaganda and trying to make the government shut this place."

The above analysis would reveal that while the LeT is the main group which has conducted the attack, links to other elements with an anti India affront also needs to be explored. The first possibility is that the LeT along with criminal elements such as the Dawood Group with or without the support of the Inter Services Intelligence (ISI) had launched the attack. The LeT does have the resources and criminal group of Dawood Ibrahim has an umbilical linkage to Mumbai being accused of the 1993, Mumbai serial blasts. The second possibility is that of the Al Qaeda and the LeT. This grouping has a larger motive of upsetting the strategic axis aligned against it which includes the Pakistan army. Another possibility is of ISI rogue elements with the LeT and the Al Qaeda being involved in the attack. Mr K Subrahmanyam states that chances of this operation which is so sophisticated in nature involving travel by sea and landing off Mumbai without the knowledge of the ISI is very slim.[11] Indian authorities have spoken of linkages with the ISI, while LeT involvement is officially accepted by Pakistani authorities with a clamp down on the camps of the terrorist group in Pakistan Occupied Kashmir after the United Nations imposed sanctions on its mother organization the Jamaat ud Dawa.

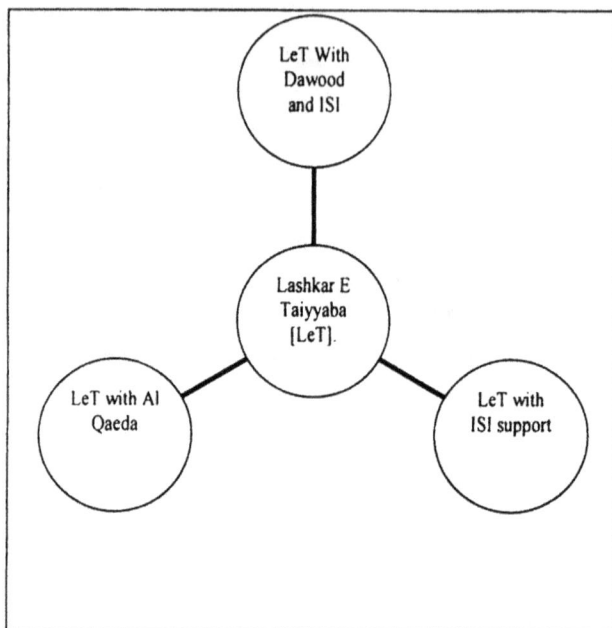

## Possible Combinations – LeT Plus

**Who is Lashkar?**

The Lashkar -e-Taiba variously referred to as the Lashkar-
e-Taiyyaba or Lashkar-e-Toiba or LeT or Lashkar is one of the
most dangerous organizations operating from Pakistan. The
Lashkar started with the aim of accession of Kashmir to Pakistan.
Thus its aim was stated as, "Merger of Jammu and Kashmir in
Pakistan".[12] Over the years the Lashkar has expanded its aim to
include a pan Indian spread. Thus the agenda as given in the

pamphlet, "Why are we Waging Jihad" considers restoration of Islamic rule over India as one of its enduring aims for the future. The objective extends even further to bringing about a union of all Islamic countries around Pakistan to include Central Asia.[13]

The Lashkar was established by two university professors from Pakistan, Hafiz Muhammad Saeed and Zafar Iqbal in 1986. Abdullah Azam associated with the International Islamic University in Islamabad and close assistant of Osama is also reported to have assisted them in setting up the organization. The role of the all pervasive Pakistani external intelligence agency the ISI in establishment of the LeT is also most significant.[14], The LeT is also one of the most extremist terrorist organizations and like the LTTE believes primarily in the tactics of suicide attacks. It has been a part of the Kashmiri terrorism grid since its raising in 1993 drawn from its root organization the Markaz ud Dawa.

The Lashkar e Taiyyaba is banned in Pakistan but has been functioning in Pakistan Occupied Kashmir where the ban does not apply. The head of this organization is Moulana Abdul Wahid Kashmiri, thereby giving it a local touch and the supreme commander is Zaki-ur Rehman Lakhvi, a master mind of the Mumbai terror attacks by many accounts. The LeT follows the Salafist ideology akin to that of the Al Qaeda, while the Pakistani establishment has been stricter on the Deobandi group, the Jaish e Mohammad.[15]

In the United States the Lashkar first came on the United States Treasury Department's Office of Foreign Asset Control (OFAC) list in the year October 2001.Thereafter it has consistently remained on the List and sustained its activities using various aliases to escape detection for short periods. The United Nations has banned the group in May 2005. However the Jamaat ud Dawa (JuD) continued to operate in Pakistan and is said to have a favourable ear of ubiquitous intelligence agency the Inter Services Intelligence (ISI). The JuD the mother organization of the LeT has also been on the list of foreign terrorist organisations in the US since 2006 and assets of its leader Mr Saeed have been frozen. But Mr Saeed addresses large gatherings in the country and the government is unwilling to control him fearing a back lash by its many followers. There are however sufficient grounds to believe that the organisation has been continuing its campaign of vituperative propaganda and hatred against India. Moves to impose ban on the JuD and Hafeez Saeed by the United Nations had not succeeded on three occasions previously primarily as China had raised technical issues.

The base organization of the Lashkar is the Markaz ud Dawa which is affiliated to the Ahl-Hadith school of reformist Islamic movement founded by Maulana Nazir Husain in northern India in the 19th Century. The focus of the Ahl Hadith School is purification of Islam which was seen to be polluted by the influence of Hindu customs and practices in India. The aim was to influence Muslims to leave Islam's practices which were not in consonance with the Quran and the Hadith or traditions. Thus a pure form of Islam was to be followed which solely relied on these preaching. The association with purity in the name of Lashkar arises from this background.

Fundamental indoctrination is a major focus of the Lashkar ideology imparted to each student forcing them to abandon their individual, clan or tribal identity. Shaving beards is thus taboo and the traditional dress of salwars or baggy trousers is a must. Each Lashkar inductee is indoctrinated with the zeal to fight for Islam and martyrdom becomes their sole purpose. Military training is an integral part of the student's curriculum and two courses are followed. A short 21 day general course called as the Daura-E-Aam and a long three month course called as the Daura-E-Khas. The training mainly focuses on techniques of guerrilla warfare of hit and run attacks, ambushes and survival drills.

The headquarters of the Lashkar is in Muridke, Gujranwala district near Lahore and its base of operation is in Muzaffarbad in Pakistan Occupied Kashmir. The Lashkar network in Pakistan is said to be extensive with over 2200 offices mostly in Punjab and recruiting centres for fighters all over the country. An Islamic school and university are run at Muridke since 1994. Here students from a large number of Muslim communities attend and smaller establishments imparting ideological indoctrination of jihad have been established in other parts as well. There are a number of training camps established and branch offices openly operating in Pakistan from where recruitment takes place. The vast network of the organization includes 135 secondary schools and 16 Islamic institutions apart from a large number of seminaries. The LeT offices are spread in all major cities extending from Muzaffarabad, Lahore, Peshawar, Islamabad, Rawalpindi, Karachi, Multan, Quetta, Gujranwala, Sialkot, Gilgit (in the Northern Area of PoK). While the LeT does not have its own web site, it uses that of its parent wing http://www.jamatuddawa.org as a platform to voice its opinions. (The web site was running till 24 Decemer 2008 despite UNSC sanctions on the organisation). There are a number of documents and newspapers published by the organisation to include Al-Dawa an Urdu Monthly, Gazwa, an Urdu weekly, Voice of Islam, an English monthly, and Al-Rabat - monthly in Arabic, Mujala-e-Tulba - Urdu monthly for students and Jehad Times - Urdu Weekly. [16]

The Chief of the LeT as has been brought out is Hafiz Muhammad Saeed, Zia-Ur-Rehman Lakhvi alias Chachaji (Supreme Commander), Yahiya Mujahid the spokesman, Abdullah Muntazer 'Spokesman for International Media' and Maulana Abdul Wahid a senior leader.[17] That the leadership is more of a family affair is also evident with Saeed's son Talha responsible for the activities in Muzaffarabad and son in law Khalid Waleed the Lahore Office. While the names of the field commanders operating in various parts including Kashmir change from time to time due to casualties, the top echelon of the leadership remains constant. Lashkar fighters have fought apart from Afghanistan in Bosnia, Chechnya, Kosovo, and the southern Philippines.[18]

The Lashkar recruits extensively from the poor and unemployed youth in Punjab particularly in the southern part of the region. The organization has been accused on buying young boys for suicide attacks promising their parents monetary rewards. A Lashkar coordinator dismissed that the organization bought the loyalty of terrorists from their parents, "Young boys come to us usually because their friends have convinced them, because they believe jihad is the epitome of being a good Muslim or because their families are involved," he said.[19] But Sharmeen Obaid, a filmmaker who has covered jihadists in Pakistan extensively, said that selling boys into jihad is a common practice. "It's happening more and more nowadays as people become more desperate for money in Pakistan," she said. "After the [2007 Kashmir] earthquake when a large number of children became orphans, I was told that a number of them were sold to organizations such as Lashkar," she added. The prce of one recruit as per Sharmeen could range from 10,000 to 19,000 dollars.[20]

The financial support network of the Lashkar is extensive. Thus it collects donations from the public at large and is known to hold promotion rallies for the purpose within Pakistan. The Lashkar's fund collection methodology has been varied and it has included placing a collection box for donations in every Pakistani town. This was being done in the name of the so called struggle in Kashmir and the public are known to have contributed liberally. These funds were supplemented by money provided by external sources as also coffers of the Pakistani intelligence agencies. It also collects donations from the ex patriate Pakistani community in other parts of the World including the Gulf, United States and United Kingdom. Many Islamic NGOs are also known to support the Lashkar. The Jamaat ud Dawa web site also solicits funds for the organization. The LeT financial management is quite modern and thus it is known to have withdrawn a large quantum of its funds from bank accounts in Pakistan once it was warned by some elements that the state was likely to freeze its accounts post 9/11. On the other hand these funds were invested in various front businesses such as commodity trading and small businesses as well as manufacturing and real estate.

The Lashkar has been at the fore front of the suicide attacks launched in Kashmir from 1999 to 2002. The bulk of the over 55 attacks launched by squads comprising of two men during this period have been attributed to the Lashkar and are primarily targeted against the police, paramilitary or army camps in Jammu and Kashmir[21] The Lashkar itself is careful not to designate its attacks as suicide missions as this form of death is not permitted in Sunni ideology but invariably calls them as daredevil missions. However the LeTs main newspaper the Jihad Times refers to the suicide bombers as fidayeen or those who dare to give their lives.[22]

## Conclusion – UN Sanctions on Jamaat ud Dawa

The survival of the LeT in Pakistan is due to the Jamaat ud Dawa factor. India made a convincing case in the wake of the Mumbai Terror strikes and the UN Security Council Committee established pursuant to paragraph 6 of resolution 1267 (1999) concerning Al-Qaida and the Taliban and associated individuals and entities added the JuD, Al Rashid Trust and Al Akhtar Trust International along with four individuals including Hafiz Muhammad Saeed to the Consolidated List imposing sanctions on the individuals and organisations.[23] Pakistan immediately ordered "closure" of all JuD offices within hours of the United Nations sanctions. A Reuters report from Islamabad said that JuD / LeT boss Hafiz Saeed, one of the four terrorists sanctioned by the UN Security Council, had been placed under house arrest in Lahore.[24] Zaki-ur-Rehman operations commander of the LeT alias Lakhvi, chief of finance Haji Muhammad Ashraf and Saudi financier Mahmoud Bahaziq are the three terrorists sanctioned by the UN Security Council.

Simultaneously other organizations involved in sustaining terrorism in Kashmir, such as the United Jihad Council (UJC) an umbrella group, formed in 1994 comprising of Harkat-ul-Ansar, Hizbul Mujahideen, Jamiat-ul-Mujahideen, Al-Jihad, Al-Barq, Ikhwan-ul-Mussalmin and Tehrik-ul-Mujahideen amongst others was also constrained. "Following the Mumbai attacks and the subsequent tension between Pakistan and India, the United Jihad Council has decided to remain silent," reported the News International quoting a commander of one of the UJC member organisations who requested anonymity.[25]

Pakistan's rapid actions were not unsurprising, for apart from UN sanctions there were strong reasons to believe that had they delayed a response, India could have well launched selective air strikes on terror bases in Pakistan and Pakistan Occupied Kashmir. The UNSC in some ways bailed out Islamabad defusing a potential crisis in the Sub Continent.

---

**(Endnotes)**

1 Foreign SIM cards, fake IDs from Bangladesh. Available at http://timesofindia.indiatimes.com/ Foreign_SIM_cards_fake_IDs_from_Bangladesh_/articleshow/3776197.cms

2 Arrests won't affect us, jihad will continue: Lashkar. Available at http://www.expressindia.com/ latest-news/Arrests-won—t-affect-us—jihad-will-continue—Lashkar/396262/

3  Praveen Swami. Terror mail analysis supports claim of Lashkar authorship . The Hindu. 1 December 2008. New Delhi p 10.

4 Lashkar came via sea from Karachi, used Gujarat boat to reach Mumbai. Available at
http://www.indianexpress.com/news/lashkar-came-via-sea-from-karachi-used-gujarat-boat-to-reach-mumbai/391642/

5 Emily Wax. Calls Shed Light on Gunmen's Motives. Available at
http://www.washingtonpost.com/wp-dyn/content/article/2008/12/15/AR2008121502717_pf.html

6 Yoginder Sikand. Islamist Militancy in Kashmir: The Case of the Lashkar-i Tayyeba. 20 November 2003. Available at http://www.sacw.net/DC/CommunalismCollection/ArticlesArchive/sikand20Nov2003.html

7 Emily Wax. Calls Shed Light on Gunmen's Motives. Available at
http://www.washingtonpost.com/wp-dyn/content/article/2008/12/15/AR2008121502717_pf.html

8 Praveen Swami. Mumbai  massacre story unfolds in terrorists interrogation. The Hindu. 2 December 2008. new Delhi p 1.

9 Praveen Swami. A journey into the Lashkar. The Hindu. 2 December 2008. New Delhi p 10.

10 Hasan Suroor. Mumbai terror Suspect's Pakistan link, "confirmed". The Hindu 8 October 2008. New Delhi. P 1.

11 K Subrahmanyam. Don't March to Their Beat. Times of India 3 December 2008. New Delhi. P 18

12 Bammi, General Y M. War Against Insurgency and Terrorism in Kashmir. Natraj. Dehradun. 2007. p 95.

13 Lashkar e Taiyyaba. Extension of Kashmir Jihad Factory. Unpublished paper by security-risks.com.

14 Tariq Ali, The Clash of Fundamentalisms: Crusades, Jihads and Modernity, Verso, London & New York, 2002, p.199.

15 Muzamil Jaleel. Why Pakistan Won't Give Up Lashkar. Sunday Indian Express. 7 December 2008. New Delhi. P 8.

16 Information accessed from the web site of the Jamaat ud Dawa. www.jamaatuddawa.org. The site was running till 24 December 2008 despite UN SC sanctions on the organization.

17 Lashkar-e-Toiba 'Army of the Pure'. Available at http:// www.satp.org/satporgtp/countries/india/states/jandk/ terrorist_outfits/lashkar_e_toiba.htm

18 Bammi, General Y M. Note 1. p 95.

19 Arrests won't affect us, jihad will continue: Lashkar. Available at http://www.expressindia.com/latest-news/Arrests-won—t-affect-us—jihad-will-continue—Lashkar/396262/

20 Ibid.

21 Bammi. Note 9. p 141.

22 Bammi. Note 9. p 142.

23 Mr. E. Ahamed, Minister of State for External Affairs at the UN Security Council on Threats to International Peace and Security Caused by Terrorist Acts. MEA India Press Release 9 December 2008. Available at www.meaindia.nic.in

24 Amit Baruah. JuD faces heat after UN ban. Available at http:// www.hindustantimes.com/StoryPage/FullcoverageStoryPage.aspx? sectionName=&id=f9fde3dd-53c5-47da-b361-eea707b4ed39 Mumbaiunderattack_Special&&Headline=Jamaat+faces+heat+after+UN+ban

25 Mazhar Tufail. Major Jihadi groups disappear. Available at http:// www.thenews.com.pk/top_story_detail.asp?Id=18922

# 5

## India Responding to Terror in Mumbai

### The Initial Response

The scale of the Mumbai attacks surpasses that of the 2001 Parliament attack and 2002 attack on the Akshardham temple in Ahmedabad. The terrorists used a combination of bombs and bullets by suicide attackers, a dangerous and a new trend in hinterland terror which was well appreciated by the establishment. The first response of the Indian government was preventive to control the conflagration. A country wide alert was announced. The area of the national capital region, New Delhi, Gujarat, Rajasthan, Bangalore, Hyderabad and Kolkata along with some areas of Uttar Pradesh were considered most vulnerable. Gujarat, Rajasthan and other metros which are frequented by foreigners and ex patriates remained the key areas of concern apart from the national capital, Delhi and were placed on a high alert. Precautions against a 9/11 type of air strike by hijacking aircraft were also taken with the Indian Air Force remaining alert specially near the national capital.

The Prime Minister Dr Man Mohan Singh addressed the nation on 27 November condemning the terror attacks, "I strongly condemn these acts of senseless violence against innocent people, including guests from foreign countries. The well-planned and well-orchestrated attacks, probably with external linkages, were intended to create a sense of panic, by choosing high profile targets and indiscriminately killing foreigners". He added that the main aim of the attackers was to create mayhem in the commercial capital thus, "It is evident that the group which carried out these attacks, based outside the country, had come with single-minded determination to create havoc in the commercial capital of the country" and assured that strongest possible measures would be taken to avoid repetition of such attacks[1]

At the apex level it is not clear if the Crisis Management Group which is headed by the Cabinet Secretary was convened immediately after information of the strike was received on the night of 26 November. The Prime Minister Man Mohan Singh is reported to have held a meeting on 28 November with the chiefs of defence services and intelligence agencies. Defence Secretary Vijay Singh, Home Secretary Madhukar Gupta, Naval Chief Admiral Sureesh Mehta, Army Chief General Deepak Kapoor, Air Force Chief Air Marshal Homi Major, Coast Guard Director General Admiral R F Contractor and Intelligence Bureau Chief P C Haldar attended the meeting.[2] The main focus of the meet was to discuss the unprecedented attacks and preventive measures to be taken. An all party meeting was also held by the Prime Minister Man Mohan Singh on 30 Nov wherein the response to Pakistan was reportedly discussed. Some of the measures outlined on subsequent days by the Prime Minister included setting up a Federal Investigation Agency (FIA), strengthening air and maritime security and creating four NSG hubs in various parts of the country.

In a political fall out, the Finance minister P Chidambaram replaced incumbent Home Minister Mr Shivraj V Patil who had earlier resigned owning moral responsibility for the Mumbai terror attacks. In the state of Maharashtra, Mr Ashok Chavan took over as the Chief Minister and Mr Chhagan Bhujbal as the Deputy Chief Minister. Given that these appointments reflect the proximity of the replacements to the political leadership of their parties, efficiencies achieved may be suspect unless the new incumbents demonstrate otherwise.

The Defence Minister AK Antony had follow up meetings with Navy chief Admiral Sureesh Mehta to review the security measures being undertaken for coastal security along India's 7,516-km long coastline. "The Defence Minister had an hour-long meeting with the Navy chief today to discuss the security situation and to seek the details of how the terrorists entered the Mumbai coast undetected to carry out the dastardly attack," Defence Ministry sources were reported by the PTI. [3] The Defence Minister is also reported to have called for greater coordination among all agencies – both Defence and Internal Security in such a way so that intelligence inputs available become actionable.

Shri Antony's comments were made in a meeting with the top brass of Ministry of Defence, attended by the three Service Chiefs – Admiral Sureesh Mehta, General Deepak Kapoor, Air Chief Marshal FH Major and the Defence Secretary Shri Vijay Singh. The meeting was called to review the security situation and state of preparedness to face any terrorist threats. The meeting also discussed the plan for coastal security and the acquisition of Systems and Platforms including Coastal Radars and Interceptor

Boats. The Defence Minister also reviewed in detail the preparedness against any possible terror threats from air. The situation along the Line of Control was also discussed including tightening of measures to prevent infiltration of terrorists given that Pak Occupied Kashmir continues to be an important area for recruitment and training of terrorists. [4]

On the diplomatic front the Prime minister had highlighted some of the proposed measures in initial speech on 27 November which included taking up the terror issue strongly with Pakistan to prevent use of territory for attacks thus, "
We will take up strongly with our neighbours that the use of their territory for launching attacks on us will not be tolerated, and that there would be a cost if suitable measures are not taken by them. We will take a number of measures to strengthen the hands of our police and intelligence authorities. We will curb the flow of funds to suspect organizations. We will restrict the entry of suspects into the country. We will go after these individuals and organizations and make sure that every perpetrator, organizer and supporter of terror, whatever his affiliation or religion may be, pays a heavy price for these cowardly and horrific acts against our people".[5]

Speaking in the Indian Parliament, India's Home Minister, Mr P Chidambaram stated, "I am, however, able to say that the finger of suspicion unmistakably points to the territory of our neighbour, Pakistan. The interrogation of the captured terrorist has yielded valuable material evidence. The origins of the ten terrorists who entered India have been established conclusively. There is also abundant evidence gathered from the inflatable rubber dinghy, the fishing vessel and the bodies of the terrorists that has enabled the investigators to reconstruct the sequence of events from the origin to the targets".[6]

In the official diplomatic response, the High Commissioner of Pakistan was called to the Ministry of External Affairs and informed that the terrorist attack on Mumbai was carried out by elements from Pakistan. The Indian Government expected that strong action would be taken against those elements, whosoever they may be, responsible for this outrage. It was conveyed to the Pakistan High Commissioner that Pakistan's actions needed to match the sentiments expressed by its leadership that it wishes to have a qualitatively new relationship with India. Concurrently it was reported that Pakistan Foreign Secretary Salman Bashir summoned Indian High Commissioner Satyabrata Pal in Islamabad to give a "response" to the Indian demarche, rejecting New Delhi's contention.[7]

India also successfully invoked provisions of UN Resolution 1267 (1999) and the Security Council Committee established pursuant to paragraph 6 concerning Al-Qaida and the Taliban and associated individuals and entities which oversees the implementation by States of the three sanctions measures, assets freeze, travel ban and arms embargo imposed by the Security Council on individuals and entities associated with the Taliban, Usama Bin Laden and the Al-Qaida organization. Speaking at the UN Security Council meet on Threats to International Peace and Security Caused by Terrorist Acts Mr. E. Ahamed, Minister of State for External Affairs called for specific measures to include the following:-

- The Jamaat-ud-Dawa and other such organizations need to be proscribed internationally and effective sanctions imposed against them. Their country of origin needs to take urgent steps to stop their functioning. A message must also go out that perpetrators of terrorist acts must be brought to book and not given sanctuaries in some states.
- Practical measures at the global and national level need to be immediately put in place to see that the menace of terror is uprooted.
- The Comprehensive Convention on International Terrorism that India tabled in 1996 needs to be adopted immediately to provide a framework of international law against terrorism. This cannot be held hostage to definitions while terrorists continue to take innocent lives.[8]

The Committee obliged by placing a ban on the Jamaat ud Dawa, its principals Hafeez Muhammad Saeed, Chief of operations, Zaid ur Rehman Lakhvi and financers Haji Muhammad Ashraf and Mohammad Ahmed Bahaziq.[9] This was at the fourth instance that such a resolution had been moved but the first time that it was passed, as China which had been blocking the same on three occasions previously raising technical grounds preferred to remain silent. Pakistani authorities claimed later that President Zardari had specifically requested the Chinese to let the resolution through.

Back home a Parliament Resolution was passed on 12 December unanimously condemning the terrorist attacks in

Mumbai by elements from Pakistan. Text of the Parliamentary Resolution is as per Appendix C.

## Priming for Military Action

By now reports in the Indian media indicated that the armed forces had been ready for a surgical strike on Pakistan and the armaments likely to be used were listed, with the Indian Air Force, the most reluctant of the three services to go to war, knowing fully its implications this time around seeming more than keen to strike. However the Defence Minister defused tensions on 16 December stating that there were no plans for military action. "We are not planning any military action...But at the same time, unless Pakistan takes action against terrorists operating from its soil against India, and also against all those behind the Mumbai attacks, things will not be normal," said Mr A K Antony.[10]

Media speculations however continued about priming of the Indian fighter jets for "offensive action" within a day or two of 26/11, but the final government go-ahead did not come. "The moment passed and then the US jumped in with assurances of making Pakistan deliver on Indian demands," said a source. The foreign media was particularly active with TV Channel CNN quoting unnamed Pentagon officials saying, IAF began "preliminary preparations" for "a possible attack". Private security risk analysis organizations again based in the USA such as Stratfor, continued to float reports of possibilities of outbreak of hostilities.[11]

Aircraft and armaments which could be used in such strikes were increasingly jargonized by the media and Mirage-2000s, Jaguars, ground-attack MiG-27MLs, laser-guided bombs and missiles, cluster and thousand-pounder bombs, "litening laser designation pods" and so on seemed to be common lexicon. Even time taken to strike once the government go ahead was given was being speculated thus, "From there, if the government directive had come with real-time intelligence about the terror camps and other targets, it would have taken a maximum of four hours to actually carry out surgical strikes across the border," said a source. These sources remained anonymous raising credibility of such reports. The possibility of employing fighters in forward bases and use of IL-78 mid-air refuellers was also discussed.[12]

A Daily Telegraph Report suggested that the army had not mobilized due to political restraint as well as advantage accruing of adoption of "cold start" doctrine, which provides offensive potential to the defensive corps of the army in conjunction with the Air Force to react across the borders. The series of exercises held to crystallize this concept which envisaged large scale mobilization by battle groups of the defensive corps also called as the pivot corps to include Divya Astra 2004, Vajra Shakti 2005 and Sanghe Shakti were summarized. The defensive corps were reportedly to create openings if required for the three strike corps, 1,2 and 21 to, "go deeper at designated targets".[13]

Meetings by the Defence Minister Mr A K Antony with the core group continued. The Minister had probably revived the periodic meetings supposed to be held with the service chiefs on a weekly basis or more frequently as the case may be during periods of crisis. The Defence Ministry was quick to issue briefs of such meetings thus, "Defence minister today (Thursday 18 December) held a meeting with the three service chiefs and defence secretary Vijay Singh to review the overall security situation and to take stock of the state of preparedness of the armed forces," defence spokesman Sitanshu Kar said in a statement. Army chief General Deepak Kapoor, navy chief Admiral Sureesh Mehta, air force chief Air Chief Marshal Fali H Major and defence secretary Vijay Singh assessed the position with regard to certain critical equipment and the status of ongoing acquisitions. "Antony emphasised the need for the forces to be fully geared up to face any challenge or threat that may arise. Security along the land and maritime borders, particularly in the light of terror threats was reviewed," Kar said.[14]

Intelligence remained the focus of these meets with the services asked to coordinate intelligence sharing. "The services were asked to put a suitable mechanism in place to ensure proper analysis and follow up of all relevant inputs. The security of vital coastal and offshore assets was discussed with a view to ensuring that these remained fully secured," Kar added.[15]

Mean while the initial positive response from Pakistan was positive with the government agreeing to send the ISI chief as requested by the Indian Prime Minister in his talks with his counter part. Thus Zahid Bashir a spokesperson was reported by the Indian Express as saying, "The two sides will work out the modalities for the visit of the Inter Services Intelligence Chief which is expected to take place soon".[16] This and the sanctions on the

Jamaat ud Dawa which were enforced by the administration perhaps lulled the Indian side into complacency of success of a strategy to carry out armed preparation and using international diplomacy to force Islamabad to clamp down on terror.

But soon the mood in Pakistan changed and the Zardari government supported by the people, a vocal media and the invisible directions of the Army reversed gears taking shelter behind the strategy of deniability. Kasab's antecedents in Pakistan were thus rejected with the Pakistan High Commissioner in New Delhi also denying the presence of Masood Azhar who had been named by the Indian side in a list of 40 submitted to Islamabad as those required to be deported to the country in a television interview with host Karan Thapar. A detailed review of this shift is being carried out in subsequent chapter, suffice to say India began to reconsider its options by around 20 December. External Affairs Minister Pranab Mukherjee indicated on 20 December that in case Pakistan failed to keep up with its assurances, the entire range of options was open.

A meeting of the Cabinet Committee of Security was held by Prime Minister Manmohan Singh on 21 December with service chiefs who are normally not a part of the Committee but can be invited in attendance. Held in the South Block office of the Prime Minister as against an office in the residence, analysts were to draw conclusions of possible military options being discussed. All this was happening as the tempo on the other side was also rising with the Pakistan Air Force flying over their main cities.

However the Indian Prime Minister attempted to defuse tensions on 23 December stating that war was not an option and terrorism was the main issue. The same day Pakistan's Chief of Army Staff, General Pervez Kayani however announced that Pakistan will react within seconds, a claim supported by media reports that Pakistan Air Force had deployed in the forward airfields.

A comprehensive analysis of the Indo Pakistan escalation is also being carried out in subsequent chapters. Suffice to say that both countries were taking maximum measures to suggest to each other that they would exercise the military option if coerced to do so. India if Pakistan did not act against the terror infra structure and Pakistan if India strikes, both sides relying on the air option.

With trip wires armed, a false alarm possibly by the terrorist group which has perpetrated the Mumbai attack could well see a slanging match in the air between the two nuclear neighbours. Thus adequate measures need to be taken behind the screen of jingoism, moving beyond the standard DGMO hot lines to avoid an inadvertent escalation.

## Impact on Business and Investment

Terror attacks leading to a possible war is a scenario most dreaded by businessmen going through a financial crisis which has led to recession in the global economy. The Mumbai terror attacks proved highly detrimental to business and foreign investments in India. Mumbai is the financial capital of the country and the prime destination for foreign investors and financiers. Mumbai's significance to the Indian economy is evident contributing 5 percent to the GDP. It has 60 percent of customs duty collections, 40 percent of foreign trade and income tax collections each and 20 percent of central excise. As hub of financial transactions it accounts for 70 percent of capital transactions and 40 percent of maritime trade. [17] Estimates of losses as per some reports were to the tune of Rs 50,000 Crore.[18]

The losses to local businesses arising from shut down due to the terror attack in Mumbai were estimated at Rs 4000 Crore.[19] "It is an overall loss of the economy as hotels, shops and all businesses were closed. A minimum of Rs 1,000 Crore per day is lost when such a shut-down takes place," Assocham Secretary D S Rawat said. "If you take the impact for four days due to the siege, then the overall loss could be over Rs 4,000 Crore," he added.

The attacks also led to India being included in the 20 most dangerous places to visit in the World along with neighbours Pakistan and Afghanistan.[20] Investors who were ready to come flocking to Mumbai thus far as the attackers had targeted primarily the middle and lower class commuters in local trains are likely to rethink their options given that 26/11 was unmistakably a strike at upper class Mumbai citizen and foreign business traveler and tourist. Thus the government was spurred to control the negative effect on priority.

The Home Minister P Chidambaram who had most recently relinquished the portfolio of the Finance Minister was conscious of the overall impact on the security as well as economy.

A meeting of chief ministers of states was thus called on 6 January to discuss the country's preparedness to prevent terror attacks.

## Conclusion

The see saw in Indo Pakistan relations over Mumbai terror continued even as India tasted initial success through the resolution in the UN Security Council banning the Jammat ud Dawa. Pakistan subtly shifted focus from accepting that the terrorists were Pakistani citizens to a situation of ambiguity where they denied and also tried to put the blame on India for the crisis. The key issue remains "evidence" of Mumbai, which India says it has and Pakistan says it wants to see. India should show Pakistan the evidence it has, but insists Pakistan needs to fulfill its pledge to move against the terrorists. The problem appears to be that both the countries do not trust each other and therefore there is always a sense of unexpected propped up by either party. Pakistan is thus soft-pedaling action against the alleged groups saying that India has not produced evidence; India is perhaps thinking Pakistan will to reject the evidence as insufficient anyway, so why present it? The media on both sides is egging on the governments who are hard put to justify their stands thereby taking at times contradictory tones.

In this ping pong battle, the terrorists have got the respite that they wanted by shifting the focus from their dastardly actions, which both sides have unequivocally condemned. The diplomatic shuffle and compulsions of Pakistan's continued denial of ownership of the attackers in Mumbai as well as other non state actors needs detailed discussion as is being carried out in subsequent chapters.

Appendix C

**Parliament Resolution on the terrorist attacks in Mumbai**
12/12/2008

THIS HOUSE

expresses its unequivocal condemnation of the heinous terrorist attacks in Mumbai by terrorist elements from Pakistan, destroying hundreds of innocent lives and seeking to destroy the values that India stands for;

Notes that this outrage follows acts of terror committed since the beginning of this year in various places across India and on the Indian Embassy in Kabul;

Notes with deep concern the fact that Lashkar-e-Toiba, a terrorist organization that is listed in the UN Security Council Resolution 1267 and is banned in Pakistan, has continued to operate and launch terrorist attacks against India;

Notes the Government's firm intention to review circumstances leading upto the attacks on Mumbai and to take further measures as may be necessary to safeguard national security;

ON BEHALF OF THE PEOPLE OF INDIA, FIRMLY RESOLVES
THAT

• India shall not cease her efforts until the terrorists and those
who have trained, funded and abetted them are exposed and
brought to justice;

• India shall firmly counter all evil designs against its unity,
sovereignty and territorial integrity;

• India will remain resolute and will be victorious in its fight
against the barbaric menace of terrorism; and

• That the ideal of a secular and democratic India shall prevail.

**(Endnotes)**

1 Prime Minister's address to the Nation. Available at http://
pib.nic.in/release/rel_print_page.asp?relid=45116

2 Mumbai attacks: PM meets chiefs of defence services. Available
at http://timesofindia.indiatimes.com/India/
PM_meets_chiefs_of_defence_services/articleshow/3773131.cms

3 Lapses in security: Antony seeks Navy to explain. Available at
http://www.expressindia.com/latest-news/Lapses-in-security-
Antony-seeks-Navy-to-explain/392886/

4 Coordinate to make available intelligence inputs actionable –
Antony to defence top brass. MOD India Press Release 3
December 2008. Available at http://mod.nic.in/

5 Prime Minister's address to the Nation. Available at http://
pib.nic.in/release/rel_print_page.asp?relid=45116

6 HM announces measures to enhance security. Available at http://
pib.nic.in/release/release.asp?relid=45446&kwd=.

7 Pak responds, summons Indian high commissioner. Available at
http://timesofindia.indiatimes.com/India/
Pak_responds_summons_Indian_high_commissioner/
rssarticleshow/3781674.cms

8 Mr. E. Ahamed, Minister of State for External Affairs at the UN
Security Council on Threats to International Peace and Security
Caused by Terrorist Acts. MEA India Press Release 9 December
2008. Available at www.meaindia.nic.

9 Security Council Al Qaida and Taliban Sanctions Committee Adds
Names of Four Individuals to Consolidated List, Amends Entries of
Three Entities. Available at http://www.un.org/News/Press/docs/
2008/sc9527.doc.htm

10 No plan for any military strike against Pak: Antony

http://timesofindia.indiatimes.com/

No_plans_of_military_action_against_Pak_Antony/articleshow/

3844285.cms

11 Was India mulling air strikes on Pak camps? Times of India

Report. Available at

http://timesofindia.indiatimes.com/India/

Was_India_mulling_air_strikes_on_Pak_camps/articleshow/

3843431.cms

12 Ibid.

13 Daily Telegraph Report by Sujan Dutta. Available at http://

www.telegraphindia.com/1081206/jsp/frontpage/story_10214744.jsp.

14 PIB MOD India Press Release 18 December 2008. Available at

mod.nic.in

15 Ibid.

16 ISI Chief on his way to outraged New Delhi. Indian Express

report. Indian Express. 29 November 2008. New Delhi. P 1.

17 Reeba Zachariah. Attacks may have cost Rs 50K Crore. The

Times of India. 1 December 2008. New Delhi. P 17.

18 Ibid.

19 Mumbai lost Rs 4k cr during attacks. Available at http://

www.indianexpress.com/news/mumbai-lost-rs-4k-cr-during-attacks/

392203/

20 Indian Express Report. India Among 20 most dangerous places

to visit. The Indian Express. 1 December 2008. p 13.

# 6

## Diplomatic Power Play

*"Given the multi-pronged initiatives India has recently taken, including isolating us in sports, is "a final solution" for Pakistan in the offing?"*

Pakistani defence and political analyst Ikram Sehgal

### General

"The terror attack in Mumbai from November 26 to 29 marked a qualitatively new and dangerous escalation of the terrorism that India has faced for over two decades. Through this period, as in the Mumbai attack, major terrorist acts in India have been sponsored and organized by groups and forces from across our borders. The Mumbai attack also made it clear that terrorism is a direct threat to international peace and security," said India's, Minister of State for External Affairs Mr. E. Ahamed at a meet of UN Security Council (UNSC) on Threats to International Peace and Security Caused by Terrorist Acts.[1] The UN body condemned the attacks in Mumbai unequivocally thereby creating space for India to utilize international approbation for harsh measures against terrorist groups operating from Pakistan.

India is not new to a situation of adversarial relationship with its neighbour caused by a terrorist attack. Indo Pakistan rivalry is now a permanent feature of the global conflict prevention discourse. There have been numerous incidents of acrimony in the past sixty years of existence of the two states. Some have led to war as in 1965 and 1971, others to limited wars localized to sectors as in 1999, while India has established that Pakistan is fanning an ongoing militancy in Kashmir. A brief survey of the flash points between India and Pakistan since independence is as per Appendix D.

Most recently in December 2001, when Pakistan based terrorist groups, Lashkar e Taiyyaba (LeT) and Jaish E Mohammad (JeM) attacked the Indian Parliament, there was similar consternation in the country for retribution against these. Pakistan failed to relent resulting in mobilization of the Indian Armed forces on the Indo-Pakistan border and the Line of Control with possibilities of war at least twice, once in January 2002 and the second time in May the same year. The net result of the stand off remains unclear as is normal in such circumstances both sides, India and Pakistan claimed to have attained their respective objectives.[2]

It is now apparent that Operation Parakram as the Indian mobilization was called then failed to provide any lessons for a future situation arising from a terrorist attack directed and coordinated from Pakistani soil. An ideal course of resolution of long standing issues including terrorism and Kashmir was never sought; instead a fait accompli exercise called as Confidence Building Measures was put into place which has yet to attain the desired momentum to bring peace to the Sub Continent. Events in 2008 would prove the same.

In July 2008, the Indian Embassy in Kabul was targeted by a suicide bomber resulting in the death of over 50 including the Indian Defence Attaché and the Press Counsellor[3]. Embassies are sovereign government space, fingers had pointed to the Inter Services Intelligence (ISI) of Pakistan.[4] In December, Mumbai happened again the needle of suspicion fell on the Lashkar at the behest of the ISI. Perhaps the only lesson learnt by the decision makers from 2002 was that mobilization without taking it to the logical conclusion of war to break the impasse of Pakistan's denial in complicity of terrorism is counter productive.[5] Thus no mobilization was ordered, while it is now apparent that a possible air strike on assets of terrorists in Pakistan Occupied Kashmir may have been contemplated. But the main focus remained on diplomacy.

Given this backdrop, India had the following possible options to engage its neighbour to attain the aim of disbandment of terror infra structure by Pakistan:-

(a) Engage Pakistan bilaterally.

(b) Influence Pakistan through the United Nations.

(c) Persuade Pakistan through intermediary powers supposedly with influence in Islamabad, namely United States and United Kingdom.

(d) Seek multilateral engagement particularly through prominent allies of Islamabad as China and Saudi Arabia.

All these options have a number of drawbacks. They need sustained pressure not just over days but months and years given the deep rooted nexus of terror in Pakistan which has seemingly seeped into all segments of society, have become geographically visible across the country and have support from a small but powerful section with fundamentalist leanings. Given that the Establishment, an euphemism generally used with reference to the Pakistan Army considers terror as a covert instrument of state policy, dismantling terror infra structure in the country would need long term action by the international community. On the contrary global politics has a limited attention span restricted to the next crisis.

Moreover concerted pressure by the United States in the past has failed to persuade Pakistan from taking sustained action against the Taliban-Al Qaeda combine lodged in its tribal areas. A recent report in the News International indicated that the Taliban had gained control of Swat, one of the two areas where operations have been undertaken by the Pakistan Army.[6] Under the circumstances it is evident that sustained pressure on Pakistan by the international community would be a long term strategy interspersed with options of surgical strikes and possibly even localized wars.

Turning to Pakistan, given the evidence available and provided by India particularly identification of the terrorist apprehended in Mumbai, traced back to his village Faridkot by the media, Pakistan also had four possible options summarized as follows:-

(a) Accept India's position and given their own admission of terrorist networks operating in the country, cooperate with India in a joint effort to counter it.

(b) Deny involvement and refuse to acknowledge terror groups operating on its soil.

(c) Accuse India of a conspiracy, raise war hysteria and exploit fears of nuclear exchange to seek international intercession in toning down Indian demands.

(d) Create situations where Indian citizens are accused of involvement in terrorist activities within Pakistan or outside thereby creating a state of ambiguity.

It would be seen that Pakistan had one positive and three negative strategies the latter based on a combination of denial, diversion and ambiguity. This triad had served Pakistani elite's interests in the past as despite US focus on war on terror since 9/11 in which Islamabad was the main ally, terrorism within Pakistan has grown manifold. There were no reasons to believe that post Mumbai there would be a change of heart. But politics and diplomacy thrives on the possible.

Now let us see how these strategies had played by end December. For this a chronological review of Indo Pakistan discourse post 26/11, created from official press releases and media reports during the period would provide an ideal start point:-

- 26 November 08 – Terror attack in Mumbai. Terrorist, "Kasab", a Pakistani citizen apprehended. Reveals LeT plot.
- 27 Nov – Pakistan government expresses regret – willing to send ISI chief.
- 28 Nov – Indian External Affairs Minister speaks to Pakistan Foreign Minister for action.
- 28 Nov– Hoax call to President Zardari.
- 29 Nov– Pakistan refuses to send ISI Chief.
- 30 Nov– India appeals to US for pressure on Pakistan.
- 1 Dec 08– Demarche issue to Pakistan. Indian foreign secretary visits US.
- 2 Dec– Senator McCain unscheduled visit to New Delhi.
- 3 Dec– US Secretary of State Visits New Delhi goes to Islamabad. US Chairman Joint Chiefs of Staff, General Mike Mullen visits Islamabad, then New Delhi.
- 5 Dec– Trade talks with Pakistan put on hold.
- 7 Dec– Pak places Laskhar military commander, Zaki ur Rehman under house arrest.
- 9 Dec– India calls for ban on Jamaat ud Dawa (JuD) in UNSC. Pakistan places Masood Azhar under house arrest later denies the same.
- 10 Dec– UNSC issues ban. Pakistan undertakes action against JuD and LeT camps and offices, places leaders under house arrest.

- 11 Dec– Indian Parliament condemns Mumbai terror attacks.
- 13 Dec– Pakistan accuses violation of air space by Indian Air Force aircraft India denies.
- 16 – 17 Dec– Pakistan denies that Kasab is a citizen, denotes that Masood Azhar is not in the country, completely retracting previous statement.
- 21Dec – Indian PM holds meeting of key security ministers and advisers.
- 22 Dec:-
  - o Pakistan provided with Kasab's statement and request to meet the Pakistan High Commissioner in New Delhi.
  - o Pakistan carries out fighter sweeps over major cities. Pakistan defence minister indicates country is ready for defending sovereignty.
  - o US Joint Chiefs of Staff visits Islamabad, for the second time during the month.
  - o Indian External Affairs Minister seeks greater transparency and avoidance of denial by Pakistan.
- 24 Dec– Pakistan National Assembly adopts a resolution stating that the nation would thwart any attempts to violate national integrity and sovereignty.
- 25 Dec:-
  - o Pakistan Prime Minister says there can be no war with India.
  - o Indian External Affairs Minister speaks to Chinese Foreign Minister on telephone.

o    Pakistan alleges that an Indian citizen Shukla is involved in a bomb blast in Lahore, apprehends him.

26 Dec:-

o    Reports in Pakistan media indicate movement of troops close to the border and shift of some formations from the West to the East.

o    Indian Prime Minister holds a meeting of top ministers and defence officials.

o    Pakistan Prime Minister denies any intent of war, seeks assistance of friendly countries to defuse tension.

An overview of the above chronology would indicate that possibly India and Pakistan have attempted all·the four options, yet no break through has been made, indeed none was possibly anticipated in such a short time given the nature of antagonistic relationship between the two states. Each of the options available to India is now being examined in detail as per succeeding paragraphs.

## Bilateral Engagement

As has already been stated elsewhere, Pakistan's initial response to the terror attack on Mumbai was cooperation and conciliation. The Prime Minister agreed to send the ISI Chief to Delhi for a joint investigation as requested by the Indian Prime Minister, some thing which would have been unprecedented in Indo Pakistan discourse. Later Pakistan whittled down stating that the demand was for a Director of ISI. Thus Zardari stated in a television interview, "We had announced that Director would come from the ISI, because it is too early for the Directors General to meet at the moment".[7] Finally as the mood changed, Islamabad completely denied that they had agreed to send a representative of the ISI. Thus having established an excellent rapport for bilateral resolution Islamabad whimpered down to tame denials and bureaucratese.

The official diplomatic dialogue started on 28 November, when the Indian External Affairs Minister spoke to the Foreign Minister of Pakistan Makhdoom Shah Mahmood Qureshi to convey the hope that the Government of Pakistan will take immediate action with regard to the terrorist attacks on Mumbai, said the Ministry of External Affairs Press Release and went on, "He conveyed that while the Government of Pakistan has said that it wants a leap forward in our bilateral relations, outrages like the attack on our Embassy in Kabul and now the attack on Mumbai are intended to make this impossible. The groups responsible and their supporters are, therefore, also acting against the direct interests of the Government of Pakistan. We expect Pakistan to honour its solemn commitments not to permit the use of its territory for terrorism against India". Later speaking in the Parliament, the External Affairs Minister clarified that this conversation was recorded in the form of Speaking Notes, thereby leaving no ambiguity in the Indian demands. The Foreign Minister of Pakistan was speaking to Indian women press corps at that time and was interrupted during his interaction showing the seriousness with which the issue was treated by Indian authorities. Mr Shah choose to cut short his visit and return to Pakistan given that the atmosphere was not conducive for him to continue normal diplomatic activities as also given the need for consultations in Islamabad.

Sensing that not much action had been forthcoming from Pakistan specific to its demands, India issued a demarche to the Pakistan High Commissioner on 1 December wherein he was categorically informed that the attack on Mumbai was carried out by elements in Pakistan and India expects strong action from the country in consonance with the statements by its leadership which had called for, "a qualitatively new relationship with India".[8] India had also reportedly asked for the deportation of Dawood, Tiger Memon and Masood Azhar.

Simultaneously Indo-Pak secretary-level talks to discuss Sir Creek issue scheduled for December 2-3 were deferred though it was later clarified that the talks had been postponed much earlier. "The talks on Sir Creek were postponed a week ago, much before the Mumbai terror," external affairs ministry spokesperson Vishnu Prakash was reported to have told the news agency IANS. Simultaneously meeting of India-Pakistan Joint Commission on Environment was also called off and visa applications of Pakistani nationals to India were to be processed in 30 days instead of the usual seven to 15 days, as per Mr Suresh Reddy, Visa Counsellor at the Indian High Commission in Islamabad.

At this juncture there was some action on the part of the Pakistani government as Zaki-ur-Rehman Lakhvi and 11 others were detained in a raid on 7 December on a LeT camp in Pakistan Occupied Kashmir. Adullah Ghazanvi confirmed that, "It was our camp and our people were arrested from there," he said.[9]

Pakistan concomitantly sought more information and evidence. Foreign secretary Salman Bashir told the Indian high commissioner Satyabrata Pal in Islamabad in a demarche that, "_____ (to) carry forward these investigations, we require detailed information/evidence. In this context, while reiterating our suggestion for joint investigations, the foreign secretary proposed that a high-level delegation from Pakistan may visit New Delhi as soon as possible."[10] It was obvious that the positive reactions initially had been diluted after considered deliberations in Islamabad.

The atmosphere for bilateral dialogue was further vitiated by allegations of a call by the Indian External Affairs Minister Mr Pranab Mukherjee which was later proved to be hoax to the Pakistani President, Mr Zardari threatening war in case Pakistan did not react positively to the Indian demands. Another curious incident related to allegations of violation of Pakistani air space by the Indian Air Force. After initial reports in the media, Pakistan called in the Dy High Commissioner in Islamabad to lodge a formal protest.

"Today morning the Pakistani Foreign Office handed to our Mission in Islamabad a Note Verbale alleging air space violations by Indian aircraft five days ago. These same allegations were first reported in the Pakistani and international media for several days and are a part of Pakistani disinformation campaign. It had been made clear by GoI when we saw the reports that no violations of Pakistani air space by Indian aircraft have taken place. This was also conveyed to the Pakistani side when the Pak DGMO raised it verbally with our DGMO on the evening of 16th December 2008, three days after the alleged violations. The Note

Verbale given by the Pakistani Foreign Office today will be examined and responded to appropriately by the Government of India," was the official Indian reaction to the allegations.[11]

On its part the IAF strongly denied the air violations. "IAF is a responsible air force of a responsible nation. There has not been any airspace violation by our aircraft," IAF spokesperson Wing Commander Mahesh Upasani said.[12] The prompt Indian denial, like the one issued after the fake "threatening phone call" that Islamabad had earlier claimed its president had received from foreign minister Pranab Mukherjee, forced Pakistani President Asif Ali Zardari to downplay the incident saying it was "not actually an airspace violation".

Despite the many misunderstandings, Zardari continued to maintain a modicum of civility and hopes for some action by his government. In an opinion piece in the New York Times on8 December he contended, "India is a mature nation and a stable democracy. Pakistanis appreciate India's democratic contributions. But as rage fueled by the Mumbai attacks catches on, Indians must pause and take a breath. India and Pakistan — and the rest of the world — must work together to track down the terrorists who caused mayhem in Mumbai, attacked New York, London and Madrid in the past, and destroyed the Marriott Hotel in Islamabad in September". Continuing to link the issue of terrorism with the cruel assassination of Benazir he wrote, "The terrorists who killed my wife are connected by ideology to these enemies of civilization".[13] To the Financial Times in a telephonic interview he stated, "The architects of this calamity in Mumbai have managed to raise a threat on our other (eastern) border. As we have these people (militants) on the run along our western border (with Afghanistan), our attention is being diverted at this critical time."[14]

When asked about the stand of the Pakistani government on dismantling the intelligence apparatus's support to terrorist groups he contended, "In the past, lots of mistakes have been made, I cannot deny that. But the present government does not support any such action — I can assure the world from my side, from my Army's side, from my parliament's side and the people of Pakistan that we are not helping any such activity."[15]

By then the pressure to act had been converted in the form of a UNSC declaration banning the Jammat ud Dawa and imposing restrictions on individuals which were acted upon. However there was a subtle shift from - acceptance of some elements in the country responsible for the attacks who would be dealt with to - Pakistani authorities harping on lack of evidence. Thus Prime Minister Gillani said, "We have yet to see evidence. They (people in India) were in a state of mind which one can expect at that time. They said in anger something but now the dust has settled down".[16]

On 22 December India gave letter from Mr Kasab to the Pakistani authorities to establish proof of his being a Pakistani citizen. "This evening the Indian Government has forwarded to the Pakistan High Commission in New Delhi a letter from one 'Mohammad Ajmal Mohammad Ameer Qasab' who claims to be a Pakistani," said a statement by Pakistan Foreign Office spokesman Mohammad Sadiq on 22 December. "He (Iman) has sought assistance of a lawyer and a meeting with the Pakistan High Commission. The contents of the letter are being examined," the statement continued.[17] Pakistani authorities continued to deny that Kasab was a citizen of the country producing electoral records to prove the case. This is not unusual in a country which has incomplete electoral rolls. For instance Punjab to which Kasab belongs has a population of over 86 million. As per the Election Commission of Pakistan, 44969427 voters were registered from Punjab for the Elections in 2008 as on 9 January.[18] With 60 percent of population generally in the voting age, a back of the envelope calculation would reveal that approximately 6 million plus or 13 percent have not been registered as voters in the province.

By now India was exasperated with the hardened attitude of Pakistani authorities. The Indian cricket tour to Pakistan was thus called off as per the Board of Cricket Control of India on the advise of the External Affairs Ministry. "The final decision has been taken. We have got the letter from the Sports Ministry and the Ministry of External Affairs not to proceed with the tour", senior BCCI official Rajeev Shukla said.[19] This was a body blow to Pakistan cricket, where no foreign team has toured over the past year.

In the interim period there was a war hysteria raised mainly through statements of leaders on both sides. Cliché's like, "all options", "we will respond instantaneously", "nuclear war", were being raised. Public anger spilled over on the streets and the media became increasingly nationalistic. The Pakistan National Assembly unanimously adopted a resolution on 24 December stating that the country was "united and stands ready to defend its honour and dignity as well as its territorial integrity" and that the nation and the armed forces shall together defend the country's security "at all costs".[20]

The atmosphere was diffused by around Christmas with the Prime Minister Gillani stating, "There is no question of war. There is absolutely no question of war. We had good relations with India. I assure you that we want excellent relations with India. We want to maintain good relations with India."[21] A day earlier the Indian prime minister had stated that war was not an option and war hysteria should not be raised to cover up inaction in bringing the terrorists to book. "My request to friends in Pakistan is to address the issue that is terrorism and not create war hysteria. They should act against those responsible for the Mumbai terrorist attacks," said Dr Manmohan Singh.[22]

Meanwhile on 25 December the bogey of Shukla, a supposedly Indian citizen responsible for bomb attacks in Lahore was floated by Pakistan, though officially nothing was conveyed to the Indian High Commission. Meanwhile a pro-Taliban group called 'Ansar Wa Mohajir' claimed responsibility for the car bomb attack in Lahore.[23] The wheel had now turned full circle. It was evident that bilateral engagement had proved of limited consequence but the need to maintain linkages despite the mood varying from outright hostility to tepidity on both sides cannot be undermined.

Indian establishment was hopeful since they had made a clear distinction that the government in Islamabad was not in the know of the terror attacks, they should accept New Delhi's position. As the External Affairs Minister stated in the Parliament, "I have never claimed, I have never accused that Pakistan Government is responsible. Very carefully, I have used the words 'elements in Pakistan'".[24] Mr Mukherjee also explained that engagement with a government which was not able to deliver was inevitable as there was no other option. "Now, whether the incumbent Government is in a position to deliver or not is not my look-out. I cannot look into it. With whom shall I have to interact? I have to interact with Foreign Minister, with President, with Prime Minister, with the established Government, not with somebody, the so-called real power behind the scene. That may be practical politics. But that is not the domain of diplomacy, and, in the international arena, I shall have to deal with established Government" he said.[25]

It would therefore be evident that bilateral engagement between India and Pakistan in an atmosphere surcharged with nationalistic sentiment on both sides cannot be expected to provide positive results. The government however had to make an effort which it did; possibly it never appreciated that once the, "Establishment" implying in this case the Pakistani Army and the Foreign Office took charge of handling Indian demands, there was no hope of a compromise. Acceptance of any demands overtly was difficult not just domestically but also internationally for that would have led to damning Pakistan as a base and supporter of terrorism. The option of disowning some of the terrorists and criminals named in the list of 40 given to Islamabad could well have been exercised but even that was foreclosed once public opinion ranted against New Delhi.

Can Pakistan do what it did to A Q Khan squarely blaming him as an individual for clandestine nuclear proliferation? Even that option does not exist given the states open association with the likes of Hafeez Saeed, who has a much larger political lobby supporting him than Khan. Similarly Dawood Ibrahim continues to be the blue eyed boy of the Pakistani intelligence agency ISI, which has arranged to move him to a safe house in the capital Islamabad, from his mansion in Karachi.[26] Dumping Zaki-ur-Rehman Lakhvi and other lesser functionaries who are openly associated with planning and conducting the terrorist attack should however be easier and could be now focused upon by India if some break through is to be made otherwise after the dust has settled it would be back to the effete CBM process.

### India's UN Option

India had an option to go to the United Nations which was exercised using the opportunity of Meeting of the UN Security Council on Threats to International Peace and Security Caused by Terrorist Acts. Mr E Ahamed, Minister of State for External placed India's demands before this authority which were accepted and the JuD, Al Rashid Trust and Al Akhtar Trust International along with four individuals including Hafiz Muhammad Saeed were added to the Consolidated List imposing sanctions on the individuals and organisations on 10 December.[27] China which had not supported such a stand on three occasions earlier did not raise any technical objections this time. Pakistan took action as per the UNSC Directive. There was uproar over the arrests dubbed officially as house arrests as also the country succumbing to outside pressure. "Pakistan should revisit its policy of bowing before international pressure immediately, without regard for the pros and cons of its actions," said Maulana Abdul Aziz Alvi JuD's head in Kashmir.[28]

What about actions beyond UN Security Council on Threats to International Peace and Security Caused by Terrorist Acts? India would have to ensure follow up and place before the Committee its impressions of compliance to the UNSC Directive by Islamabad. These would remain contentious with Pakistan placing its point of view. Going beyond this, Praful Bidwai a noted columnist and peace activist has suggested use of the United Nations Security Council Resolution 1373, which requires all states to "refrain from providing ... support... to entities or persons involved in terrorist acts...", give "early warning to other states" and "deny safe haven to those who finance, plan, support, or commit terrorist acts..." —all on pain of punitive measures to pin down Pakistan.[29] Menaka Guruswamy an advocate also talks in similar vein.[30] In addition she also recommends invocation of the UN Security Council Resolution 1566 on criminal acts resulting in death or provoking terror is not justifiable under any circumstances.[31] She recommends that the Indian government should raise these provisions to force the Pakistani and also the Saudi government to stop financing terror groups and support their infra structure. Mr N Ram, influential editor of the Hindu also proposes adoption of the UN 1373 route, despite its possible fall out of being linked to the Kashmir issue.[32] A copy of the UN Security Council Resolution 1373 (2001) dated 28 September 2001 is as per Appendix E.

There are problems in practical implementation of the UN option. Things in the UN do not work in strictly legalistic terms with politics having an important role to play. Pakistan's all weather friend China would not allow any further damnation of Islamabad, thus unless a proposal has been worked out with the P5 in the United Nations, it is likely to be rejected. The Indian government also turned to the US to put pressure on Pakistan as is discussed in subsequent paragraphs.

**Engaging Pakistan through the US**

The United States administration under George W Bush is on its last legs and it would prefer to avoid intervening in a possible conflict in the Sub Continent. However given intractability of Indo Pakistan dialogue and consequences of a scale up, United States soon entered the scene. In what could perhaps be the last assignment as Secretary of State, Condoleezza Rice rushed to the Sub Continent on 3 December 2008 attempting to defuse tensions. Her first visit was to New Delhi where she met the government and political leadership including Mr L K Advani, the opposition leader in the parliament. In a press release the US Embassy clarified that, "Her visit is in the context of the terrorist attack in Mumbai that had targeted innocent civilians including tourists from all parts of the world. Both President Bush and Secretary Rice have been in telephonic contact with PM and EAM since November 27, 2008 and have offered any assistance that India may need".[33] Ms Rice focused on three issues prefixed with the adjective, "real" transparency, sense of action and urgency. "What has to happen is there has to be a real sense of transparency, real sense of action and real sense of urgency because these are

extremists who have the same intention and same goal and that
is to terrorise and send message to states around the world," she
told reporters.[34] "I have said that Pakistan needs to act with
resolve and urgency and cooperate fully and transparently. That
message has been delivered and will be delivered to Pakistan"
said Dr. Rice.[35] She added: "What we are emphasizing to the
Pakistani government is the need to follow the evidence wherever
it leads and to do so in the most committed and firmest possible
way." The US Joint Chiefs of Staff, Mr Mike Mullens was at the
same time on a reverse circuit visiting Islamabad and then
followed up to Delhi.

Not withstanding these assertions, the leverages that
India and the US have to constrain Pakistan remain limited and
need to be reviewed in tandem. Sumit Ganguly a well known and
respected authority on South Asia based in the US believes that
Pakistan is not likely to cooperate with India. In the pursuit of
asymmetric warfare strategy followed by Pakistan feels Ganguly,
partial cooperation with Indian authorities is in built. This is
borne by abandonment of the LeT and the Jaish e Mohammad
post the attack on the Indian Parliament in December 2001 and
their subsequent revival once the pressure was off. Sustained US
pressure remains the only way out as per Ganguly.[36]

George Friedman CEO Strategic Forecasting believes that
Pakistan government has a serious credibility problem. "The
Pakistani government is even weaker than the Indian
government. Pakistan's civilian regime does not control the
Pakistani military, and therefore does not control the ISI. The
civilians can't decide to transform Pakistani security, and the

military is not inclined to make this transformation", writes Friedman in "Strategic Motivations For Mumbai Attack" on his web site www.stratfor.com.

So how far US pressure on Islamabad works remains to be seen. It apparently did not work during Operation Parakram when as per Lt Gen Retd V K Sood and Pravin Sawhney, "India relied completely on the US in the belief that the, "two democracies" had a common fight against international terrorism".[37] An outgoing Bush administration may not be able to extract promises from the Pakistani government and the Obama administration would perhaps be too new to the job even though the State department will be led by high profile Ms Hillary Clinton. Till the Administration settles down after what is usual jockeying for relative power between its various arms some initiatives can be expected. On the other hand for India this may also raise fears of greater acquiescence to the US in the country, restraining New Delhi's flexibility domestically. As senior BJP leader Arun Shourie said in the Rajya Sabha recently, "Please stop running to mummy (US) hoping that somebody else will help the country to tackle terrorism."[38]

## Multilateral Engagement

The nature of the Mumbai attack, involvement of a large number of foreigners and the loss of 26 lives implied a wave of sympathy from the international community. After expression of condolences attention was focused on avoiding an Indo Pakistan confrontation. The European Union with many members deploying troops in Afghanistan under the aegis of the NATO/

ISAF combine also appealed for peace. Gerard Araud, Director General of Political Affairs in the French Ministry of Foreign Affairs and European Affairs stated, "We expect Pakistan to cooperate fully in this investigation. We consider it very important." China added its voice to the large number of nations calling for dialogue and bilateral cooperation. Foreign Ministry spokesman Liu Jianchao stated in response to a question during a routine foreign office briefing, "It is also in line with the requirements for regional peace and stability and the common expectation of the international community."[39] Beyond that there were limited leverages that the international community as a whole is able to exercise over Pakistan, linking assistance by the International Monetary Fund to tangible measures could be one, though this would have to be examined in greater detail. While there is much talk in India about trade and travel barriers including a possible revocation of the Indus Water Treaty of 1960, these would hurt both sides and may not serve the desired purpose of bringing the Establishment to book terrorists and their groupings.

Indian government possibly believed that China could exercise influence, hence there were reports that India's External Affairs Minister spoke to China's Foreign Minister Mr Yang Jeichi on 25 December and in a 30 minute talk conveyed that Pakistan was not doing enough to clamp down on the terrorist infrastructure in the country. This was the first high level exchange with Beijing and was also followed up with a talk with US secretary of state Condoleezza Rice explained as a, "courtesy Christmas call" in a report by Manini Chatterjee of the Daily Telegraph on 26 December.[40] While China has enough leverage with Islamabad, it may be wary of treading into a domain which has multiple dimensions geopolitical, regional and bilateral. A nuanced response would therefore be expected from Beijing though the initiative by Mukherjee was worth the effort.

The circle of influence on Pakistan was expanded the next day with India appealing to Saudi Arabia during the most opportune visit of the HRH Prince Saud Al-Faisal Foreign Minister of Riyadh to New Delhi on 26 December. Iranian Foreign Minister Manouchehr Mottaki also reportedly rang up Mukherjee on the same day and conveyed Tehran's support to New Delhi against terrorism in the region. Saudi Arabia is a key ally of Pakistan and has enormous clout over the powers-that-be in that country. Saudi agencies are also known to be a base of monetary assistance through numerous trusts to the terror groups. Thus engagement of Saudi Arabia is important. Iran's solidarity is also important for India, however tangible results from the engagement need to fructify.

**Concluding Remarks**

India's demands on Pakistan have been specific, hand over the terrorists identified, close the terror infra structure and assist in investigating the Mumbai terror strike bringing the culprits to book. Pakistan after an initial wave of cooperation and closing down the Jamaat-ud-Dawa in a half hearted manner has taken the route of deniability. Denying that Kasab was a Pakistani citizen, that Masood Azhar was in the country and that the ISI or the Pakistani army was in any way responsible for the terror strikes on India or supporting the infra structure. On the other hand Islamabad is seen by New Delhi to side track the issue by raising war frenzy, focusing global attention on avoiding a conventional conflict leading to a possible nuclear exchange as also holding the threat of diversion of troops from the Eastern front operating against the Taliban thereby placing NATO in Afghanistan under pressure. Pakistani perception is that India is not sharing enough credible evidence, which was supported by the Interpol Chief during his visit to New Delhi and Islamabad recently. India is wary that any information shared such as the statement by Kasab recently would be rejected outright.

Even domestically anti India sentiment in Pakistan has grown creating pressure not to act against the terrorists and groups named by New Delhi. Many opinion makers who would normally advise moderation are now speaking of harder options, "Our strategic reserves, presently employed in FATA, Swat and Bajaur, must be redeployed immediately to our eastern borders. Vacillation amounts to gambling with this nation's existence, irresponsibility bordering on criminal negligence," wrote Ikram Sehgal adding, "We must have peace with India, war is not an option. Unfortunately, if it means demeaning one's national self-respect, peace fades out as a viable option and we must go to "battle stations."[41] As if on cue, news reports on 26 December indicated that there was redeployment of troops in Pakistan from the Western to the Eastern borders opposite India. Is Pakistan attempting its own version of coercive diplomacy through forward deployment one wonders? The aim of this coercive diplomacy could be designed expressly with the any or all of the purposes:-

- Create war hysteria to divert attention from the present focus on terrorism emanating from the country. This is expected to prevent pressure from the international community to force Pakistan to accede to India's requests and create leverages thereof.

- Create pressure on the US and NATO to seek India to give up or tone down its demands by using what many have described as a black mail strategy of pull out of troops acting as a lever to seek concessions from India via the US which is extremely wary of such a move given its implications on the situation in Afghanistan.

- Ward off any chance of an Indian, "surgical strike" talks of which was in the air with even the Indian Air Force Western Air Command chief indicating the large number of targets in Pakistan that the IAF had drawn up recently. The mobilisation could thus be viewed as preventive against any punitive strike option by India.

Coercive diplomacy may not remain restricted to troop deployment as the risk of escalation arises from any inadvertent moves by the lower units and formations which may lead to up grading the scale of tensions. Given this atmosphere of mistrust, the diplomatic option would remain one with many ups and downs. Examination of the Indo Pakistan escalation-de escalation matrix in this contest would be important and is being carried out in subsequent chapters.

Appendix D


## Brief Survey of Flashpoints and Flare-ups in India-Pakistan ties


      A summary of past incidents when India and Pakistan relations have reached a boiling point based on news agency Reuters and other reports is as follows:-


• Aug. 14, 1947: Pakistan formed from partition of India at end of British colonial rule, amid bloodletting between Hindus and Muslims.

• Oct 1947: The two countries fight their first war over Kashmir, after its Hindu ruler opts to join secular India rather than Islamic Pakistan.

• Jan 1949: U.N. Security Council-ordered ceasefire takes effect in Kashmir.

• Sept. 1965: Second war over Kashmir region. Combat ends after U.N. calls for ceasefire.

• Dec. 1971: Third India-Pakistan war over East Pakistan. It ends with surrender of 90,000 Pakistani troops and leads to creation of Bangladesh, formerly East Pakistan.

• Dec 1989: Jammu and Kashmir Liberation Front terrorists kidnap daughter of Indian home minister, demand five separatist leaders are freed for her release. The government gives in, in a move seen as a major boost for separatist groups.

• Jan 1990 – 2008: More than 40,000 people are reported killed in ensuing insurgency. India says Pakistan arms and trains guerrillas. Islamabad denies the charge.

- May 1998: Soon after nationalist-led alliance takes power, India holds its first nuclear tests in Rajasthan, near Pakistan border. Pakistan responds with six tests.
- June 1999: Pakistan intrudes in Kargil in Jammu and Kashmir. Indian forces evict intrusion and restore the Line of Control.
- Dec. 2001: Gunmen attack Indian parliament. India blames Pakistan-based Kashmiri militants, Pakistan denies this. India cuts air, rail and road links and pulls out diplomatic staff.
- Jan 2002: India masses troops on border. Pakistan follows suit, raising spectre of another war.
- Nov. 2002: Pakistan announces ceasefire in Kashmir. India accepts and truce takes effect on Nov. 26.
- June 2004: The two agree to set up nuclear hotline, renew ban on nuclear testing, re-open Karachi and Bombay consulates and restore size of New Delhi and Islamabad embassies.
- July 2006: Bomb blasts in India's financial capital Mumbai kill 187 people. Peace talks are cancelled after Indian government blames Pakistan-based militants.
- Sept 2008: Indian Prime Minister Man Mohan Singh and then Pakistan President Pervez Musharraf agree to resume dialogue.
- Nov 26 – 28, 2008: Attackers launch wave of gun and grenade assaults on Mumbai landmarks, killing 172 in ensuing fire fights.
- Nov 27,2008: Prime Minister Singh accuses militant groups based in India's neighbours, carried out the Mumbai assaults. Pakistani Prime Minister Yousaf Raza Gilani condemns the attacks, and Pakistan-based Lashkar-e-Taiba militant group denies playing any role in the bloodshed.
- Dec 4,2008: US Secretary of State Ms Condoleeza Rice visits New Delhi and Islamabad to defuse tension.

• Dec 8, 2008 – Pakistan cracks down on a camp of the Jamaat ud Dawa, mother organization of the LeT and arrests the main accused of master minding the terror attack on Mumbai.[42]

• December 2008 – Stand off between India and Pakistan over support to terror groups by the latter continues.

## UN Security Council Resolution 1373 (2001)

September 28, 2001

The Security Council,

Reaffirming its resolutions 1269 (1999) of 19 October 1999 and 1368 (2001) of 12 September 2001,

Reaffirming also its unequivocal condemnation of the terrorist attacks which took place in New York, Washington, D.C., and Pennsylvania on 11 September 2001, and expressing its determination to prevent all such acts,

Reaffirming further that such acts, like any act of international terrorism, constitute a threat to international peace and security,

Reaffirming the inherent right of individual or collective self-defence as recognized by the Charter of the United Nations as reiterated in resolution 1368 (2001),

Reaffirming the need to combat by all means, in accordance with the Charter of the United Nations, threats to international peace and security caused by terrorist acts,

Deeply concerned by the increase, in various regions of the world, of acts of terrorism motivated by intolerance or extremism,

Calling on States to work together urgently to prevent and suppress terrorist acts, including through increased cooperation and full implementation of the relevant international conventions relating to terrorism,

Recognizing the need for States to complement international cooperation by taking additional measures to prevent and suppress, in their territories through all lawful means, the financing and preparation of any acts of terrorism,

Reaffirming the principle established by the General Assembly in its declaration of October 1970 (resolution 2625 (XXV)) and reiterated by the Security Council in its resolution 1189 (1998) of 13 August 1998, namely that every State has the duty to refrain from organizing, instigating, assisting or participating in terrorist acts in another State or acquiescing in organized activities within its territory directed towards the commission of such acts,

Acting under Chapter VII of the Charter of the United Nations,

1. Decides that all States shall:

(a) Prevent and suppress the financing of terrorist acts;

(b) Criminalize the wilful provision or collection, by any means, directly or indirectly, of funds by their nationals or in their territories with the intention that the funds should be used, or in the knowledge that they are to be used, in order to carry out terrorist acts;

(c) Freeze without delay funds and other financial assets or economic resources of persons who commit, or attempt to commit, terrorist acts or participate in or facilitate the commission of terrorist acts; of entities owned or controlled directly or indirectly by such persons; and of persons and entities acting on behalf of, or at the direction of such persons and entities, including funds derived or generated from property owned or controlled directly or indirectly by such persons and associated persons and entities;

(d) Prohibit their nationals or any persons and entities within their territories from making any funds, financial assets or economic resources or financial or other related services available, directly or indirectly, for the benefit of persons who commit or attempt to commit or facilitate or participate in the commission of terrorist acts, of entities owned or controlled, directly or indirectly, by such persons and of persons and entities acting on behalf of or at the direction of such persons;

2. Decides also that all States shall:

(a) Refrain from providing any form of support, active or passive, to entities or persons involved in terrorist acts, including by suppressing recruitment of members of terrorist groups and eliminating the supply of weapons to terrorists;

(b) Take the necessary steps to prevent the commission of terrorist acts, including by provision of early warning to other States by exchange of information;

(c) Deny safe haven to those who finance, plan, support, or commit terrorist acts, or provide safe havens;

(d) Prevent those who finance, plan, facilitate or commit terrorist acts from using their respective territories for those purposes against other States or their citizens;

(e) Ensure that any person who participates in the financing, planning, preparation or perpetration of terrorist acts or in supporting terrorist acts is brought to justice and ensure that, in addition to any other measures against them, such terrorist acts are established as serious criminal offences in domestic laws and regulations and that the punishment duly reflects the seriousness of such terrorist acts;

(f) Afford one another the greatest measure of assistance in connection with criminal investigations or criminal proceedings relating to the financing or support of terrorist acts, including assistance in obtaining evidence in their possession necessary for the proceedings;

(g) Prevent the movement of terrorists or terrorist groups by effective border controls and controls on issuance of identity papers and travel documents, and through measures for preventing counterfeiting, forgery or fraudulent use of identity papers and travel documents;

3. Calls upon all States to:

(a) Find ways of intensifying and accelerating the exchange of operational information, especially regarding actions or movements of terrorist persons or networks; forged or falsified travel documents; traffic in arms, explosives or sensitive materials; use of communications technologies by terrorist groups; and the threat posed by the possession of weapons of mass destruction by terrorist groups;

(b) Exchange information in accordance with international and domestic law and cooperate on administrative and judicial matters to prevent the commission of terrorist acts;

(c) Cooperate, particularly through bilateral and multilateral arrangements and agreements, to prevent and suppress terrorist attacks and take action against perpetrators of such acts;

(d) Become parties as soon as possible to the relevant international conventions and protocols relating to terrorism, including the International Convention for the Suppression of the Financing of Terrorism of 9 December 1999;

(e) Increase cooperation and fully implement the relevant international conventions and protocols relating to terrorism and Security Council resolutions 1269 (1999) and 1368 (2001);

(f) Take appropriate measures in conformity with the relevant provisions of national and international law, including international standards of human rights, before granting refugee status, for the purpose of ensuring that the asylum seeker has not planned, facilitated or participated in the commission of terrorist acts;

(g) Ensure, in conformity with international law, that refugee status is not abused by the perpetrators, organizers or facilitators of terrorist acts, and that claims of political motivation are not recognized as grounds for refusing requests for the extradition of alleged terrorists;

4. Notes with concern the close connection between international terrorism and transnational organized crime, illicit drugs, money-laundering, illegal arms-trafficking, and illegal movement of nuclear, chemical, biological and other potentially deadly materials, and in this regard emphasizes the need to enhance coordination of efforts on national, subregional, regional and international levels in order to strengthen a global response to this serious challenge and threat to international security;

5. Declares that acts, methods, and practices of terrorism are contrary to the purposes and principles of the United Nations and that knowingly financing, planning and inciting terrorist acts are also contrary to the purposes and principles of the United Nations;

6. Decides to establish, in accordance with rule 28 of its provisional rules of procedure, a Committee of the Security Council, consisting of all the members of the Council, to monitor implementation of this resolution, with the assistance of appropriate expertise, and calls upon all States to report to the Committee, no later than 90 days from the date of adoption of this resolution and thereafter

according to a timetable to be proposed by the Committee, on the steps they have taken to implement this resolution;

7. Directs the Committee to delineate its tasks, submit a work programme within 30 days of the adoption of this resolution, and to consider the support it requires, in consultation with the Secretary-General;

8. Expresses its determination to take all necessary steps in order to ensure the full implementation of this resolution, in accordance with its responsibilities under the Charter;

9. Decides to remain seized of this matter.

**(Endnotes)**

1 Mr. E. Ahamed, Minister of State for External Affairs at the UN Security Council on Threats to International Peace and Security Caused by Terrorist Acts. MEA India Press Release 9 December 2008. Available at www.meaindia.nic.

2 Lt Gen (Retd) V K Sood. Pravin Sawhney. Operation Parakram : The War Unfinished. Sage, New Delhi 2003. P 59.

3 IFS officer, Brigadier killed in Kabul blast I 41killed. CNN-IBN Report. Available http://ibnlive.in.com/news/ifs-officer-brig-among-indians-killed-in-blast/68453-2.html

4 Mark Mazzetti. Eric Schimitt. Pakistanis Aided Attack in Kabul, U.S. Officials Say. Available at http://www.nytimes.com/2008/08/01/world/asia/01pstan.html?_r=1&em

5 Lt Gen (Retd) V K Sood. Pravin Sawhney. Operation Parakram : The War Unfinished. Sage, New Delhi 2003. P 89.

6 The Fall of Swat. The News International Pakistan. Available at http://www.thenews.com.pk/daily_detail.asp?id=154012

7 Too early for Directors General to Meet : Zardari. The Hindu Report. The Hindu. 30 November 2008. New Delhi. P 1.

8 On the calling in of the High Commissioner of Pakistan today evening. MEA India Press Release. Available at http://meaindia.nic.in/

9 Security forces take over Lashkar camp, says witness on 7 dec. Available           at           http://www.dailytimes.com.pk/default.asp?page=2008\12\08\story_8-12-2008_pg1_4

10 Pak refuses to hand over Dawood, Memon and Masood Azhar. Available at http://news.in.msn.com/ international/article.aspx?cp-documentid=1718560

11 Response by Official Spokesperson to a question on alleged Pakistani air space violations. Available at http://meaindia.nic.in/

12 IAF denies Pak claims of airspace violation. Times of India Report. Available at http://timesofindia.indiatimes.com/India/IAF_denies_Pak_claims_of_airspace_violation/articleshow/3836763.cms

13 Asif Ali Zardari. The Terrorists Want to Destroy Pakistan, Too. New York Times. 8 December 2008. Available at http://www.nytimes.com/2008/12/09/opinion/09zardari.html.

14 M S Tanvir. Non-state actors pose danger of war: Zardari Prince Karim urges Pak, India to iron out differences. Available at http://pakobserver.net/200812/02/news/topstories01.asp

15 Mumbai attackers are stateless actors, says Zardari. Available at http://timesofindia.indiatimes.com/articleshow/msid-3787556,prtpage-1.cms

16 'Militants can precipitate war'. News International Report. Available at http://www.thenews.com.pk/top_story_detail.asp?Id=18727

17 India gives Kasab's 'letter' to Pakistan. Daily Times Report 23 December 2008. Available at http://www.dailytimes.com.pk/default.asp?page=2008\12\23\story_23-12-2008_pg1_8

18 No of Registered Voters in respect Of Punjab Province. Available at http://www.ecp.gov.pk/content/Voters_Punjab_NA.pdf

19 India calls off cricket tour of Pak. Available at http://indiapost.com/article/sports/4903/

20 Manini Chatterjee. Daily Telegraph Report. Available at http://www.telegraphindia.com/1081226/jsp/frontpage/story_10303840.jsp.

21 No war with India, says Gilani, as Pakistan nets 'Indian spy'. India Today Report. Available at http://indiatoday.digitaltoday.in/index.php?option=com_content&task=view&id=23589&sectionid=4&Itemid=1&issueid=85

22 Manini Chatterjee. Daily Telegraph Report. Available at

http://www.telegraphindia.com/1081226/jsp/frontpage/story_10303840.jsp

23 Pro-Taliban group claims responsibility for Lahore blast: Report. Times of India Report. Available at http://timesofindia.indiatimes.com/Pak_Taliban_claims_responsibility_for_Lahore_blast/articleshow/3893906.cms.

24 External Affairs Minister's intervention during discussion in Rajya Sabha on the recent Terror Attack in Mumbai. Available at http://www.indianembassy.org.cn/press/20081215-2.htm.

25 External Affairs Minister's intervention during discussion in Rajya Sabha on the recent Terror Attack in Mumbai. Available at http://www.indianembassy.org.cn/press/20081215-2.htm.

26 S Balkrishnan. Dawood has a quiet birthday in Islamabad. Available at http://timesofindia.indiatimes.com/India/Dawood_has_a_quiet_birthday_in_Islamabad/articleshow/3898440.cms.

27 Security Council Al Qaida and Taliban Sanctions Committee Adds Names of Four Individuals to Consolidated List, Amends Entries of Three Entities. Available at http://www.un.org/News/Press/docs/2008/sc9527.doc.htm

28 Nasir Jaffry. Lock on Dawa stirs quake-zone protest - Swoop widens, silence on ban. Available at http://www.telegraphindia.com/1081213/jsp/nation/story_10246743.jsp

29 Praful Bidwai. Mumbai: overcoming denial. Available at http://www.thenews.com.pk/print1.asp?id=150897

30 Menaka Guruswamy. Financing Terror : The Lashkar and Beyond. The Hindu. 5 December 2008. New Delhi. P 10.

31 Menaka Guruswamy. Financing Terror : The Lashkar and Beyond. The Hindu. 5 December 2008. New Delhi. P 10.

32 The Hindu Report. Use UN Security Council Resolution — —. The Hindu 8 October 2008. New Delhi. P 11.

33 Press Conference in New Delhi, December 3, 2008 Available at http://www.state.gov/secretary/rm/2008/12/112606.htm

34 Press Conference in New Delhi, December 3, 2008 Available at http://www.state.gov/secretary/rm/2008/12/112606.htm

35 Rice urges Pakistan to cooperate 'fully, transparently'. News International Report. Available at http://www.thenews.com.pk/top_story_detail.asp?Id=18769

36 Sumit Ganguly. Pakistan will not cooperate with India despite US efforts. The Mint. 6 December 2008. New Delhi. P 9.

37 Lt Gen (Retd) V K Sood. Pravin Sawhney. Operation Parakram : The War Unfinished. Sage, New Delhi 2003. P 10.

38 Stop running to 'mummy' US for tackling terror, BJP to Govt. Indian Express Report. Available at http://www.expressindia.com/latest-news/Stop-running-to-mummy-US-for-tackling-terror-BJP-to-Govt/397242/

39 China appeals India, Pak to cooperate after Mumbai attacks. Available at http://newsx.com/story/37251

40 Manini Chatterjee. Daily Telegraph Report. Available at http://www.telegraphindia.com/1081226/jsp/frontpage/story_10303840.jsp

41 Ikram Sehgal. Battle Stations? Available at http://www.thenews.com.pk/print1.asp?id=153694

42 Time Line : Flashpoints and flare-ups in India-Pakistan ties. The Reuters Report. Available at http://www.reuters.com/article/worldNews/idUSTRE4AR26920081128.

# 7

## Indo Pakistan – Escalation – De-escalation Matrix

*"The political government is serious. The political government knows that it will get no space to operate if the radical right is in partnership with the military. So it wants to crack down,"*

Pakistan's Security analyst Ayesha Siddiqa

### The Signs of Armageddon

Post Christmas, winter fog characteristic in most parts of the north in the Sub Continent was penetrated by the wheels of military vehicles and rumblings of tanks on the borders in India and Pakistan. Media reports were rife with movement of military in the deserts in Rajasthan to the fields of Punjab. "Whatever movement is being reported is normal for this season," an officer at Indian army headquarters was quoted by the Daily Telegraph, "This is the time when we have exercises and a certain amount of movement takes place." [1] The Border Security Force the trip wire had observed what was called as "unusual movement" on the other side in Rajasthan.[2] And as television channels flashed photographs of smartly turned out Indian Air Force pilots entering cockpits of fighter aircraft, the Pakistani side reacted with air sorties on their own cities, raising the beat of war. It was a strange move by Pakistan Air Force, signaling war to its own people an obvious attempt to create hysteria. As Hermann Goering said, "Naturally the common people don't want war; ___. But after all, it is the leaders of the country who determine policy, and it is always a simple matter to drag the people along, whether it is a democracy, or a fascist dictatorship, or a parliament, or a communist dictatorship. ____ . All you have to do is to tell them they are being attacked, and denounce the pacifists for lack of patriotism and exposing the country to danger. It works the same in any country."[3]

Reports of move of Pakistani formations from the Western borders to Sialkot and Lahore were also circulated. An Associate Press reporter even counted the vehicles, 40 moving out of a particular camp in the West. Of the 100,000 Pakistani troops in the tribal areas, 20,000 were being redeployed. In New Delhi, the Cabinet Committee on Security (CCS) met thrice on 28 November, 21 December and 26 December, if media reports can be deciphered accurately as these were categorized as meetings by the Prime Minister with the defence chiefs in the presence of ministers of External Affairs, Defence and Home. The Defence Minister is holding regular meetings with the Chiefs of Staff, an oddity in the Indian system for though such a meet is mandated at least once a week, in normal times, Service Chiefs as a body is unlikely to get an audience with the Defence Minister on a regular basis.

In Pakistan similar meetings are being held by the Prime Minister with the service chiefs, unusual too for Islamabad where the Army Chief has been in power over the past decade or so just a few months back and the Director General Inter Services Public Relations, a two star army general has the tacit authority of overruling statements by cabinet ministers. Even the defence minister surfaced in Pakistan, not many people knew he existed; such is the aura surrounding the Army brass.

Certainly these are unusual times as India-Pakistan stand off over terrorism grows over the days. Yet both sides do not seem to be keen to go to war. So what is the hierarchy of escalation and de-escalation between India and Pakistan? A brief review of the past may provide us some clues

## Past Escalation Paradigms

War and mobilization is not strange in the context of Indo Pakistan relations. Both the countries have been to war thrice while border skirmishes are common though there has been a cease fire on the Line of Control for the past few years. The first Indo Pakistan War was fought in 1947-48. The conflict zone was restricted to Jammu and Kashmir. While conflagration in the form of mass communal killings commenced post Independence in August 1947, it was on 27 October that the Indian Army entered Jammu and Kashmir after raiders from Pakistan had ravaged the Valley and were on the gates of Srinagar. Thus it took almost two months plus for the conflict to erupt. The Cease Fire came almost a year later in January 1949 under the aegis of the United Nations.

The next war came in September 1965, but portends were evident in March in the Rann of Kutch. Thus a six months period of posturing preceded the war which was fought across the Indian Western front. Cease fire was negotiated by then Soviet Union at Tashkent in February 1965. The War in 1971 which led to liberation of Bangladesh also had a long gestation period. With refugees pouring from then East Pakistan, Indira Gandhi called in her Chief of the Army Staff and ordered him to launch an offensive in March

1971. General later Field Marshal Manekshaw felt the Army was not fully prepared for war and sought time. Thus hostilities broke out on 3 December, indicating a period of ten months of intercession. The Shimla Agreement in July 1972 was the first bilateral agreement between India and Pakistan which led to return of over 90,000 Prisoners of war by New Delhi and establishment of Line of Control as a de facto International Border.

For 18 years there was relative piece not withstanding stand offs during Brass tacks and other exercises in the 1980's and sparring on the Line of Control. In 1999, Indian troops deployed in the Kargil sector of Ladakh region of Jammu and Kashmir noticed intrusion by Pakistani forces on the Line of Control in May. Operations for eviction were under taken in June and the Pakistani forces were ejected and mediation between India and Pakistan facilitated by the United States. Pakistan had initially denoted that the intrusion was by Kashmiri militants but the lie was exposed with identification cards and bodies of troops of the Northern Light Infantry, a regiment of the Pakistani army. By then the strategic space for conflict had been constrained by acquisition of declared nuclear weapons capability by both sides.

The next conflagration was thus to denote a new paradigm in Indo Pakistani military stand offs. Known as Operation Parakram, it entailed mobilization of the Indian Army after a terrorist attack on the Indian Parliament on 13 December 2001. This was ordered on 18 December, just five days after the attack.[4] The deployment on the Line of Control and the International Border lasted for almost a year and peace was finally brokered by the United States. India contemplated aggression twice during this period, once in the first week of January 2002

and the second time in May the same year. A brief chronology of
events during Operation Parakram would be of interest:-

- 13 December 2001 – Terrorist attack on Indian
  Parliament.
- 14 December – Government blames Pakistan based LeT
  and JeM. JeM finally involved.
- 14 December – Demarche issued to Pak.
- 18 December – Troop Mobilisation ordered.
- 11 January 2002 – Indian Army Chief Announces ready
  for war.
- 12 January – Pak President issues conciliatory
  statement.
- 13 January – India welcomes Pak President's statement
  awaits concrete action – deployment continues.
- 18 January 2002 – US Secretary of State Visits India and
  Pakistan. Measures to deescalate continue.
- 14 May – Re-escalation of tension with terror attack on
  Indian army family quarters in Jammu.
- 18 May – India expels Pakistan ambassador to New
  Delhi.
- July – De-escalation.
- November – Strategic re location of troops ordered by
  India with cease fire on the Line of Control.

Operation Parakram was categorized as a Coercive
Diplomacy, posing a threat of war through military mobilization
to attain strategic aims. A lesson learnt which seems to have been
applied in 2008 is that this warning should be credible. Thus if
mobilization is ordered a nation needs to be prepared to go to
war. A study of the past escalations would also reveal that there
has been no uniform pattern in the two nations going to war. In
terms of time, this has varied from a minimum period of one

month in 1999 to ten months in 1971, when military preparations were undertaken in consonance with efforts to make peace. On the other hand apart from 1971, peace broking has been either through third party intervention such as the former Soviet Union and the United States or the United Nations.

## 2008 – Coercive Diplomacy II

While the attack on the Indian Parliament in December 2001 had been construed as the ultimate cnallenge to the Indian state, the government of the day wanted a maximum response but had to end up with a sub optimal military deployment option. In 2008, post Mumbai 26/11, the Indian government has restrained from deployment of the Army. The complicity of Pakistan in terrorism over the years, global consensus on this issue, irrefutable proof of Pakistani citizens involved in the attack with the apprehension of Mr Kasab, international isolation of Pakistan in UNSC and need to keep Pakistani civilian government in being are probably some of the reasons which have led the government not to repeat Operation Parakram.

A nuanced approach has also been taken with India's perception of distinguishing between the Pakistani 'political' government from the establishment supporting terrorism. International condemnation of Pakistan based terrorist groups and individuals have substantiated India's aggressive diplomacy. So far India has achieved the aim of Islamabad clamping down on Jamaat ud Dawa due to UN strictures. Yet the road ahead remains unclear. India wants Pakistan to give a commitment of demobilizing terrorist groups on a sustained and verifiable basis. India as well as the international community wants Pakistan should give up terror as a policy tool in the Sub Continent.

There are no indications from Islamabad of any genuine efforts to dismantle the terror infra structure so far after the initial clamp down on the Lashkar e Taiyyaba and the Jamaat ud Dawa. On the other hand what is forth coming is denial and diversion through the war option. As noted analyst and M J Akbar remarks in the Sunday Times of India on 28 December 2008, "Pakistan's generals are proving to be excellent tacticians. They have manoeuvered impressively through the terror crisis to emerge with the local Taliban on one hand arm and the Pentagon on the other" by their duplicity and double dealing with the US generals who are offering, "free pass to Pak involvement in Mumbai".[5]

Thus there is a long haul ahead and India would either have to back off or keep the powder dry. The challenge of terrorism from Pakistan is so grave that New Delhi has to sustain the diplomatic offensive and supplement it with economic, cultural, trade and communication adjuncts to cajole and coerce Islamabad to restrain terror or finally go to war. Under these circumstances what are the escalation and de-escalation scenarios in the days ahead? These are being discussed as per succeeding paragraphs.

### Escalation Matrix

The standard escalation matrix entails measures taken in various fields such as diplomatic, economic, culture and sports, transportation, military and so on. In the diplomatic field issuing Note Verbale, Demarche, engaging principal political leadership, expelling diplomats and recalling own, stalling the peace process and Confidence Building Mechanism, closure of consulates and embassies, restricting visas for citizens and finally breaking off diplomatic relations are some of the options normally used. It would be seen that some of these steps such as demarche and slowing of the peace process have already been taken by both sides.

In the Economic field, breaking off trade talks, enhancing trade restrictions, stoppage of border trade, cutting off trade relations, delaying international aid and assistance and so on are some of the many tools available. Economic sanctions if imposed by major states as United States or the European Union can be effective, for India the leverage is limited given low volume of economic engagement with Pakistan.

In addition India needs to lobby with the United States for suspension of military assistance to Pakistan. The current arrangement for annual military aid expires on September 30, 2009 end of US fiscal year 2008-09. This was part of an overall $3.2 billion US aid package agreed upon in 2003, evenly divided between military and economic assistance. However doubts over accounting of the $6.7 billion paid to Pakistan since 2001 by the United States as Coalition Support Funds (CSF) funds have been raised in a report by the Congressional Research Service (CRS) alleging mismanagement. As per Pentagon documents $6.7 billion or an average of $79 million per month has been disbursed to Pakistan since 2001, roughly 80 percent of CSF funds and equal to one-quarter of Pakistan's total military expenditures. Now it is proposed to increase the allotment by $300 million per year or roughly $ 25 million per month which will be a 30 percent increase. The US government can block the same in case Pakistan does not comply with India's requests for dismantling the terror infrastructure provided New Delhi is able to convince Washington on this account.

On the trade front, Preliminary reports indicate that Indo Pakistan trade has not been impacted so far, but border trade which had been started in Kashmir has come to a halt. More over the present movement of goods is based on contracts signed earlier. Any fresh contracts are likely to be delayed though no fresh inputs are available. At the same time there is no dire dependency by either of the countries on goods from the other, thus leverages in this field are limited. While in the field of culture and sports, blocking cultural and sports contacts and people to people interaction is envisaged. Cancellation of the Indian cricket test team's tour to Pakistan has already taken place; people to people movement between the two countries has also reduced considerably with air and rail passengers going down by half, though communication links are open.

In the field of Transportation cutting off air, rail and road links and over flying rights are some of the measures which can be identified which when spread into the field of information and communications would include restrictions on telephone communications and media controls.

In the military field, revocation of cease fire, warnings, mobilisation, movement to battle stations, UAVs and surveillance flights, small arms fire, artillery exchange, launching Special Forces, surgical air strikes, sea blockades and so on would be some of the steps leading to an all out war. There is no sequence of implementation of these measures. Thus surgical air strikes could precede violation of cease fire. Yet blockade from the sea would be an extreme step taken just before open hostilities.

Finally coming on to what the global community is most worried about, nuclear escalation. India has a declared, "no first use policy" and hence would not be the first to use nuclear weapons. Pakistan has indicated its red lines in terms of space, military, economic and political thresholds. Given by Lt General Khalid Kidwai in January 2002 as head of Pakistan's Strategic Plans Division, a position he continues to hold even today, in an interview, the same have been defined as follows[6]:-

- Space threshold - India attacks Pakistan and conquers a large part of its territory.
- Military threshold - India destroys a large part either of its land or air forces.
- Economic threshold - India proceeds to economically strangulate Pakistan.
- Domestic destabilization - India pushes Pakistan to political destabilization or creates large-scale internal subversion in Pakistan.

For India the options in immediate terms for attaining its objectives through military escalation are limited. While there are some reports that surgical strikes by fighter aircraft were contemplated, these would have been justified on terrorist camps in Pakistan. At this point, one month after the Mumbai strike, these camps would have been dismantled at least temporarily and could even be made into exclusively civilian sanctuaries resulting in collateral damage which would not be acceptable to the international community. More over New Delhi would have to be prepared for a possible retaliation. If India undertakes a short war, military objectives may not be achievable while it may strengthen the nationalist feeling in Pakistan working in favour of army and against the civilian government, thereby attaining an opposite result.

But not taking any action with terror infra structure continuing across the border, reports of sanctuary to the likes of Dawood Ibrahim and Indian government facing general elections may be difficult as the state will be seen as weak domestically as well as internationally. On the other hand a belligerent response would deprive it of international sympathy of being a victim of terrorist aggression while weakening the civilian government's tenuous hold in Pakistan. So it is a Hobson's choice for New Delhi. The Indian establishment is paying for neglect of the threat of terrorism from Pakistan over the years and not evolving viable options to overcome standard tactics of denial and diversion by Islamabad.

But war cannot be forsaken by India as an option until Pakistan shows positive signs of transforming from a country which is using terror as an external policy tool to that of a responsible state of the international community. New Delhi needs to keep the powder dry and continue to build up opinion across the World for military action. War would be well justified in the face of stonewalling tactics by the Pakistani establishment. Thus just as in 1971, India would have to create diplomatic atmosphere for armed offensive action.

Short of war, hope lies in an internal surge against terrorism and fundamentalism in Pakistan. As an editorial in the News International wrote recently, "If there is a true commitment to doing away with forces like the JuD, ___much more needs to be done. We need to expose the true nature of these forces before people; to reveal how they have lured vulnerable young teenagers away from homes and families only to turn them into killers; how they have exploited religion to further their own interests."[7] This would have to be a long term approach with the aim of shoring up the large but silent majority in Pakistan which is sick of living in a state supporting terrorism. As the Dawn writes, "What the Mumbai assault has done in this country is divert attention from the internal threat to an external 'enemy'. This must not be allowed to happen. Soul-searching is in order, and an acceptance of the fact that Pakistan is indeed a hub of militancy and terrorism. It is sad, on one level, that it has taken external pressure to stir the government into acting against those who are besmirching our name in the world. We face isolation, and internal ruin, if the common enemy is not brought to book. We have a collective responsibility to look inwards."[8]

Thus internal restructuring of policies and institutions generated by opinion makers with a balanced approach in Islamabad can lead to change. As the Frontier Post writes, "The rightist leadership, if it views the situation objectively, would surely agree that Jaishes, Lashkars and jihadis have not only brought infamy to this country globally and disrepute internationally."[9] If this positive sentiment persists in the cacophony of denials engineered by the Pakistani establishment, there is still hope ahead.

India can contribute to a change in tactics by the Pakistani establishment by supporting these sane voices and hardening its counter terror infrastructure by creating a cast iron shield of deterrence against terrorist attacks. If the targets are sufficiently difficult to strike, terror as an option loses its value. But for this to happen, New Delhi has to be prepared for far sterner measures than the perfunctory one's announced by the government in the wake of Mumbai strikes. The approach would have to be that of a nation at war against terror. The people will have to be prepared for many hardships if they want to live in peace without the fear of the Kasab's in the future.

In the diplomatic field India would have to sustain the battle alone as the international community has already got its next flash point, Gaza and is diverting its diplomatic energies to contain conflict in the Middle East. On the other hand China is emerging as a power broker in the region. Chinese Vice Foreign Minister He Yafei was in Islamabad calling for a, "need to de-escalate and avoid conflict in the interest of peace and security." This visit followed a talk by the Chinese Foreign Minister with India's External Affairs Minister, Mr Pranab Mukherjee on Christmas Day, 25 December. "Conflict is not the solution of the problem as it will only strengthen the hands of terrorists and extremists," Yafei was quoted by the media. As if on cue, a statement from the Pakistan Army indicated, "The Chief of Army Staff highlighted the need to de-escalate and avoid conflict in the interest of peace and security in the region," exemplifying the enormous clout exercised by Beijing. Will these words be translated on the ground remains to be seen? But Beijing has demonstrated that it has the leverages to contain the Pakistani authorities, particularly the all powerful army leadership.

The path of de-escalation would be dictated by the Pakistani elites decision that non state terrorist groups are not in national interest whether operating in or out of country. Both sides would then resolve outstanding disputes through the existing processes of CBMs in a time bound manner. Pakistan's financial position may also force the establishment to take some positive steps, for war would only add to its present economic deficit of spiraling inflation and lack of foreign reserves. Military and other aid can be made conditional to measurable achievements in reduction of the fundamental and extremist grid in the country.

Finally it is the ability of India and Pakistan to resolve issues through dialogue by building trust which will see lasting peace. For this ironically opposite approaches may be required, demilitarising Pakistani strategic culture while increasing security consciousness of India's political leadership.

**(Endnotes)**

1 Border flurry on both sides. Daily Telegraph Report. Available at http://www.telegraphindia.com/1081226/jsp/frontpage/story_10303841.jsp].

2 Ibid.

3 Hermann Goering. Available at http://www.wisdomquotes.com/001993.html

4 Lt Gen (Retd) V K Sood. Pravin Sawhney. Operation Parakram : The War Unfinished. Sage. New Delhi. 2003. p 10.

5 M J Akbar. How a mouse in Pakistan became its Man of the Year. Sunday Times of India. 28 December 2008. New Delhi. P 18.

6 Kaushik Kapisthalam. Pakistan leaves arms calling card. Available at http://www.atimes.com/atimes/South_Asia/GB10Df06.html

7 The JuD connection. The News International Pakistan Editorial. Available at http://www.thenews.com.pk/daily_detail.asp?id=151596

8 The common enemy. The Dawn Editorial. Available at http://www.dawn.com/2008/12/13/ed.htm

9 Avijit Ghosh. Major jihadi groups have disappeared, says Pak newspaper. Available at http://timesofindia.indiatimes.com/India/Major_jihadi_groups_have_disappeared_says_Pak_newspaper/articleshow/3833224.cms

# 8

## Will Pakistan Dismantle the Terror Infrastructure?

### Innocence or Naiveté?

Will Pakistan dismantle the terror infrastructure? This question is increasingly engaging the international strategic community today. India and Afghanistan are two states most affected by terrorist groups based in Pakistan, but there are others too. These include countries ranging from the United States to Iran and Russia, the latter with Lashkar accused of training fighters for Chechnya.[1] Iran has already suffered from Jundullah's activities in the Sistan-Balochistan province and Tehran's diplomats are routinely targeted by terrorist groups operating from Pakistan. The United States and allies of the North Atlantic Treaty Organisation (NATO)/International Security Assistance Force (ISAF) combine operating in Afghanistan which have deployed close to 50,000 troops and aid workers in the country are also concerned about their security. More over activities of groups as the LeT are stretching out to Europe, with Denmark, Germany and most recently France having detected their trail.

The initial response from Pakistan to Mumbai 26/11 as has been brought out earlier was positive. On 27 November,

Pakistani President Asif Ali Zardari telephoned India's prime minister to condemn attacks in Mumbai and suggested "non-state actors", were responsible. The Indian Prime Minister Man Mohan Singh on the other hand blamed militant groups based in India's neighbours, alluding to Pakistan. In general, Pakistani initial reaction to the Mumbai terrorist attack was a wave of sympathy but as insinuations of involvement of terror groups and the Inter Services Intelligence (ISI) was made by New Delhi; there were strong denials by the government. The public mood was also sullen and the strategy of denial was persisted until proof of involvement of Pakistani citizens in the attack with the terrorist captured being traced back to his village, Faridkot in Punjab, Pakistan emerged. This and other evidence provided by the Indian side through the US and international sources led to tacit acceptance by Islamabad that a non state actor was involved in the strike. Thus a report in the Hindu on 8 December 2008 indicated that Pakistan had cracked down on the office of the Jamaat ud Dawa, front of the Lashkar and arrested 20 cadres.[2] This was before the UNSC imposed sanctions on the Jamaat ud Dawa on 10 December.

The bottom line of the Pakistan government throughout the discourse by the establishment in the country at this stage was to focus on involvement of non state actors in the strike. Speaking to the Financial Times Pakistan President Asif Zardari squarely blamed the attacks on non state actors, "Even if the militants are linked to Lashkar-e-Taiba, who do you think we are fighting?" asked Zardari. "We live in troubled times where non-state actors have taken us to war before, whether it is the case of those who perpetrated (the) 9/11 or contributed to the escalation of the situation in Iraq," said Zardari.[3] He continued to stress on Pakistan being a victim of terrorist violence.[4]

Whether these initial responses were the genuine sentiment in the political class particularly the Pakistan People's Party (PPP) which a year back had seen its charismatic leader perish in a multiple suicide attack or temporary disconnect between the political parties and the Army which holds the reins of strategy towards India is not clear at present. But the attacks brought into focus the sharp divide between the army and the ruling government in Pakistan. The demand for the chief of the ISI to visit India to share intelligence was accepted by the Prime Minister of Pakistan in the initial burst of sympathy. But Pakistan Army spokesman, Maj. General Athar Abbas immediately reacted stating there is a need to avoid blame game and castigated Indian authorities for being irresponsible and baseless. With the army and the government speaking in two voices, civil military relations suffered a temporary set back. The Pakistan People's Party government had been increasingly seen appropriating power to the civil authorities undertaking measures such as abolishing the National Security Council and divesting the ISI of a role in internal politics in the country. Mumbai terror attacks provided the Army an opportunity to stop this tide of civilian control. At the same time given the nationalist sentiment the Pakistan army was instantly resurrected in the minds of the people and the Zardari government had to give in to the people's mood and do what the army dictates or make way for another regime as per Nirupama Subramanian of the Hindu reporting from Islamabad.[5]

Soon thus the mood changed in Islamabad. Pakistan government held a National Security Conference (NSC). The leaders strongly condemned the terrorist attacks in Mumbai but also asked Indian leadership and the media to exercise restraint while making statements. A meeting of the top security brass in Islamabad by the Prime Minister on 6 December concluded that, "unless India provides solid proof of involvement of any Pakistani non-state actor in the Mumbai attacks," Pakistan would not take any precipitate action against vague allegations. Chaired by the Prime Minister Yousaf Raza Gillani, the meeting was attended by Defence Minister Ch Ahmed Mukhtar, Foreign Minister Shah Mahmood Qureshi Chief of the Army Staff Gen Ashfaq Parvez Kayani and DG ISI Lt Gen Ahmad Shuja Pasha.[6]

Efforts to diffuse tensions and prevent deployment of forces on the borders however continued. Maj-Gen Athar Abbas, spokesman for the Inter-Services Public Relations, reaffirmed on 30 November that there was no extraordinary movement on the borders. "These are media speculations without any base and truth about the troops movement and suspension of ceasefire (on the Kashmir border)," Abbas said.[7] After a Corps Commanders meeting the Army Chief Kayani was quoted as saying, "Pakistan Army stood for peace and security."[8] The US Commander of NATO forces in Afghanistan Major General Michael Tucker, also gave a similar view on 5 December, "We stay in close dialogue with our Pakistani military counterparts in that regard, but to date we have not seen any reduction. They've told us that they're remaining committed ... to their fight here on the western side of their border," Tucker said.[9]

On the other hand the Tehreek e Taliban (TTP) in a burst of "patriotism" reportedly sought a cease fire and the Army also showed some signs of willingness to consider Baitullah Mehsud and Maulvi Fazlullah, as "patriotic" Pakistanis as per influential Pakistani journalist Hamid Mir. [10] But this bonhomie appeared to be short lived as the terrorists continued their campaign of mayhem, targeting innocents in Peshawar killing 22 in a suicide bomb attack on 6 December. Over the next two days, over 250 vehicles carrying supplies to NATO forces in Afghanistan were burnt down.

Post Christmas, there were moves to shift troops from the Western border fighting the Taliban and the Al Qaeda to the East ostensibly to thwart any Indian challenge, despite categorical rejection of any mobilization and movement of troops by New Delhi. The Pakistani response seemed to be to avoid the, "executive" action demanded by India to stem the terrorist groups and rely on deniability and diversion of war to deflect international opinion. The government in Pakistan would have to take all stake holders on board including the Army and go in for a major policy shift to see that the country no longer harbours any terrorist groups. This will no doubt be a tall order but the PPP has the commitment and the strength to do so to ensure that the so called strategic assets – the terror groups are controlled and thereafter dismantled. It is now up to the Pakistan Army leadership led by General Kayani to take up the final call. For in Pakistan the general belief is that there are two governments at work, the political led by Zardari and the Establishment which actually calls the shots on these issues led by Kiyani. Thus the burning question is resolve and determination of the Pakistani

Establishment to come to grips with terrorism emanating from its borders. We start by examining the political space in Pakistan.

**The Political Space in Pakistan**

There are three entities which are influential in Pakistan, the political parties, the army and terrorist groups. While the world has lauded the government of Pakistan People's Party (PPP) and Mr Zardari as a democratically elected one, it is the weakest of the three as political parties in Pakistan are for ever riddled with controversies, conspiracies and differences. This political space is thus naturally divided on legitimacy of the war against the TTP. It is said to be fought between one Pakistan and another Pakistan. Zardari, Musharraf, the MQM, Kayani, Asfandyar Wali supported the war against the Taliban, Jaish, Lashkar, Baitullah Mehsud, Lal Masjid.[11] As is common in such situations some of the opposition leaders are neutrals which in this case included Nawaz Sharif, Imran Khan, Qazi Hussain Ahmed, Hameed Gul, Fazlur Rehman.[12] These fissures certainly affected the response of the government. But for any fundamental change in policy there has to be a consensus between the political parties and the army. Pakistani polity is also in a crisis with confrontation building with the judiciary. The case pertaining to alleged favour shown to the daughter of the Chief Justice of Pakistan Hamid Dogar by giving her supplementary marks was being investigated by a parliamentary committee. However the Supreme Court ruled that the case was sub judice and the National Assembly Standing Committee on Education investigating the issue was ordered to cease inquiry. The Standing Committee's Chairman, Mr Abid Sher Ali, member of the Pakistan Muslim League Nawaz refused to accept the Supreme Court's "stay" order thus denoting potential of conflict between the legislature and the judiciary in the future.[13]

Seeing a political opening, opposition parties led by Nawaz Sharif are seen to join forces with the PML Q a party created and propped up by former dictator Pervez Musharraf. He was the first political leader to confirm in a round about way that Kasab was a Pakistani citizen, what the government has been denying constantly. "I have checked myself. His (Ajmal Amir Iman alias Ajmal Kasab) house and village has been cordoned off by the security agencies. His parents are not allowed to meet anybody. I don't understand why it has been done."[14] While Mr Sharif's statements can be dismissed as that of political power play between him and the PPP or Mr Zardari, it raises serious doubts of the ability of the democratic forces in Pakistan to shape the strategic space.

The second and some say the most important institution in the country is the Army. General Ashfaq Pervez Kayani, Pakistan's chief of army staff, has thus been listed at No 20 by Newsweek in a list of 50 "Global Elite". Gen Kayani's citation reads, "Kayani ... is responsible for Pakistan's nukes; for the battle against Al Qaeda and its tribal allies along the Afghan border; and for managing tensions with neighbour India".[15] With a weak political culture and lack of effective governance, the Army is seen by many as the only instrument of the state which can deliver despite the many wrongs perpetrated by the previous Army Chief Pervez Musharraf during tne Emergencies imposed in 2007. The Army retains an iron grip over state instruments and is also seen to direct the strategic space dictating the regional agenda particularly with reference to Afghanistan and Kashmir. The Army also controls the powerful Inter Services Intelligence (ISI) technically working under the Prime Minister.

The ISI is accused of being a state within a state linked inextricably with the third pressure group, the militants. While ISI and the Army have consistently denied such linkages they are frequently accused of using terrorist groups as an instrument of instability in Afghanistan and Kashmir. More over former ISI chiefs such as Hamid Gul and many middle and junior level operatives are alleged to be maintaining links with such organisations raised in the 1980's to fight the Mujahideen war in Afghanistan.

The Mumbai terror attacks were a complicated operation requiring training in a number of fighting disciplines, from navigation on the high seas to communications, hostage taking and extremist motivation. These could not have been launched by the Lashkar without the support of external elements. These could be the Pakistan Army, the ISI and the Al Qaeda.

In case Pakistan Army or the ISI are implicated, it is necessary to examine if Pakistani political government was in the know of a possible plan by the ISI-Army combine? After the Kargil 1999 intrusion by Islamabad, there was widespread speculation in the Sub Continent if then Prime Minister, Mr Nawaz Sharif was informed about the intrusion. A similar speculation is now in the air. Available indications are that the government was not in the know of such a strike, for its initial responses such as willingness to send the Director General ISI were spontaneous.

Pakistan foreign minister Shah Mehmood Qureshi, was on a visit to India. The terrorist attacks happened at the most inopportune time for him. The visibly distressed minister had to terminate his visit on 28 November after widespread charges of involvement of Pakistan. This would also indicate that he was not in the know unless this was a deliberate ploy. On the other hand it may substantiate the theory that the forces that planned the attack also had the aim of creating a cleavage between the civil and the military in Islamabad.

Respected defence and security analyst, Mr K Subrahmanyam writing in the Times of India believes that when the Pakistani political elite is insisting that they had nothing to do with the terror attacks, they may well be, "speaking the truth."[16] Thus the focus of the Indian government has also been not to implicate the Zardari government in the strikes. However there are strong beliefs that the Establishment meaning the Army and the ISI would be in the overall loop of the Lashkar plan, for without active support if not encouragement training for a maritime attack on such a large scale would have been difficult to organize.

## The Fundamentalist Space in Pakistan – Demand Factors for Terrorism

For extremism and fundamentalism to survive in a country demand factors implying ideological support are divided society and factionalism are essential. The extended influence of fundamentalism in Pakistan has been most aptly described by Mr Hussain Haqqani, noted journalist and commentator who is

presently the Ambassador of Pakistan in the United States.
Writing on, "The Ideologies of South Asian Jihadi Groups" in 2005
he states,

> "The organized jihadi movements that have been
> militarily active since the anti- Soviet Afghan Jihad can
> be classied into three groups. The rest of these groups is
> centered on the Jamaat-e-Islami (Islamic Society) founded
> by Islamist scholar ` Maulana Abul Ala Maududi in 1941.
> The second group includes the Deobandi movements that
> arose from the austere interpretations of Islam emanating
> from the Deoband madrasa of Northern India, which was
> founded in 1867 to protect Muslims from being seduced
> by Western materialism. The third group of South Asian
> jihadis is Wahhabi, which is inuenced by the doctrine of
> Muhammad ibn-Abdul Wahhab and almost invariably
> funded by Saudi Arabia". [17]

The Jamaat-e-Islami is an umbrella organization like the
Muslim Brotherhood in Egypt and is a key force polarizing
followers of Islam from the West building its base on Islamic
revivalism. The Jamaat-e-Islami does not like to be associated
with terrorism but has, "actively participated in the militancy in
Jammu and Kashmir with the full backing of Pakistan's inter-
Services Intelligence (ISI) and the Pakistan military".[18] The Hizbul
Mujahideen (The Party of Holy Warriors) which operates in
Jammu and Kashmir and comprises primarily of elements from
the state is known to have the patronage of the Jamaat's branch
based in Kashmir. The Lashkar-e- Taiba (The Army of the Pure)
on the other hand follows Wahhabi ideology and is known to be

supported by, "Saudi money and protected by Pakistani intelligence services — Pakistani authorities have been reluctant to move against either Lashkar, which continues to operate in Kashmir, or Jamaat-ul-Dawa, which operates freely in Pakistan".[19] The third grouping which follows the Deobandi ideology similar to that adopted by the Taliban is the Jaish-e-Muhammad (Army of Muhammad) led by Maulana Masood Azhar, who has been indicated as not traceable by the Pakistani government post 26/11.

With three parallel forces of fundamentalism operating in the country, reaching out to the grass roots, it would be evident that there are strong demand factors for terrorism in the country. For the Pakistani government to stand up against the ideology of the Jamaat, Wahhabis or Deobandis is a major challenge. A government may not be able to survive if it opposes the fundamentalists. Thus Pakistani political parties have been content at compromising with these forces from time to time, only the nature and degree of cooperation varies from that of a nexus during the time of Pakistan Muslim League Qaid (PML Q) or the King's party and a tacit one when the Pakistan People's Party (PPP) which is considered secular is in power. Then the many divisions in society on sectarian (Sunni – Shia) and economic lines also provide enough recruits who are motivated by poverty and lack of esteem in society to join terrorist groups. Thus demand factors will continue to drive terrorism in Pakistan.

### The Terrorist Space in Pakistan – The Supply Factors for Terrorism

The supply factors of any militancy are the terrorist groups and their infrastructure which provides the leadership, personnel, training, weapons, the planning and executing infra structure for the attacks. The militant groups in Pakistan can be divided broadly into four categories. The first is the Al Qaeda, with its global militancy perspective, the Tehreek e Taliban (TTP) comprising mainly Pashtun tribal of the Western frontier focusing on the war in Afghanistan but increasingly extending influence even up to Karachi is the second. The Lashkar e Taiyyaba with its mother organization the Jamaat ud Dawa and the Jaish e Mohammad primarily directed towards a terror campaign against India focused on Kashmir is the third group. The fourth and the final cluster comprise of Sunni groups such as the Sipaha e Saheba and Lashkar e Jhangvi which are involved in sectarian violence. Of these the first two, the Al Qaeda and the TTP are fighting as much against the Pakistan state as the United States. The LeT and the JeM are part of the larger Al Qaeda fraternity and the axis known as the International Islamic Front and are primarily directed against India. Noted counter terrorism expert, Rohan Gunaratna however states that the Lashkar e Taiyyaba has expanded its focus from a pan Kashmiri or pan Indian approach to a global one.[20]

The attacks in Mumbai have a strong Al Qaeda connection replicating tactics employed by the organization. These were well planned and strategically targeted operations with suicide attacks at multiple points, with varied tactics of bombs, grenades, indiscriminate firing and hostage taking. Ayaz Amir writing in the News International Pakistan on 05 December states that while it may not be clear so far if the Al Qaeda was involved in the Mumbai attacks or not, the methodology of assault and consequences leading to disrupting the peace process between India and Pakistan which was seen as a threat to Al Qaeda's brand of terror would have been welcomed by Osama bin Laden or his second-in-command, Ayman Al Zawahiri.[21] Rohan Gunaratna also talks of a possible link based on the operational tactics used in the Mumbai attacks to Al Qaeda.

The Al Qaeda was under pressure in Western parts of Pakistan along the Afghan frontier and a rift between India and Pakistan would imply that the Pakistan Army whose "heart was never in this fight in which it found itself engaged only because of overwhelming American pressure" as per Amir would shift its focus to the Eastern frontier. The situation thus suited the Al Qaeda for if the Pakistan Army shifts the 5 divisions deployed in the Federally Administered Tribal Area (FATA) and North West Frontier Province (NWFP), it would provide freedom to the militants to operate with impunity and also disrupt the war in Afghanistan.[22] Influential columnist, Ahmed Rashid argues that the Al Qaeda has used the attacks to create a strategic diversion employing the LeT one of its principal surrogates. He feels that this is a replication of the December 2001 attack on the Parliament which had resulted in mobilisation of Indian and Pakistani forces on the borders thereby providing a relief to the Al Qaeda in 2002 as it retreated from Afghanistan. The Al Qaeda entrenched itself in the frontier regions of Pakistan, subsequently raising the ante in Afghanistan.[23]

Amir recalls that the Al Qaeda is known to make such strategic plays, for instance the Madrid train bombings split the US coalition in Iraq by forcing Spain to withdraw.[24] Amir also finds the duo of Zardari and Gillani relatively inexperienced in responding to such situations and calls for institutionalized mechanisms rather than personal initiatives to deal with sophistication rather than emotion. His words carry some weight given the faux pas reported by the Dawn of President Zardari receiving a hoax call purportedly from the External Affairs Minister of India, Mr Pranab Mukherjee on 28 November, threatening an attack if Pakistan does not take immediate action.

Fred Burton and Ben West, writing in Stratfor.com's report, "From the New York Landmarks Plot to the Mumbai Attack", compare the Mumbai strike with a failed plot which targeted Manhattan in July 1993 planned by the Al Qaeda at a time when it was a relatively unknown organization. Dubbed as the, "Landmarks plot", it was planned to target prominent hotels in Manhattan with eight terrorists charging the Island with automatic rifles, grenades and improvised explosive devices (IEDs) so as to kill maximum people. Waldorf-Astoria, St. Regis and U.N. Plaza hotels, the Lincoln and Holland tunnels, and a midtown Manhattan waterfront heliport were some of the targets considered by the terrorists.[25]

Ria Novosti, the Russian state news agency on 27 November a day after the attack brought out a report quoting an official, "The Russian secret services have information that certain groups that have carried out attacks in Mumbai have contacts with Al-Qaeda. This includes the Lashkar-i-Tayyiba terrorist group. Fighters from this group undergo special training in Al-

Qaeda camps, located on the border between Pakistan and India."
26

The LeT's potential and capabilities have been discussed in detail in Chapter 4. It is increasingly evident that the Pakistan government has not only lost the control over activities of the non state actors but also territory. The caliphates and emirates springing up in FATA and NWFP under leaders as Mangal Bagh and Baitullah Mehsud have larger connotations for the states survival. Their operations shift from Afghanistan to Pakistan and vice versa and are now seen to challenge the NATO forces. The withdrawal of Pakistani forces from the Western borders has been reported starting 25 December. Such a move benefits two organizations, the Al Qaeda which was under considerable pressure over the past one year or so with the presence of Pakistani troops if not actual operations in the tribal area and Predator strikes by the US. Depletion in their numbers would benefit it substantially. The second beneficiary is the Pakistan Army. Reports emanating from Pakistan indicate that despite a sustained campaign of over one year, the Army has not been able to establish control over the tribal areas as well as Swat Valley, known as Switzerland of Pakistan. The News International has gone so far as to indicate that the fundamentalists have regained control in the province and issued a ban on girls attending school. The beleaguered Army would have suffered a loss of face had it continued on the Western border. The India bogie provides it an option to redeem itself in some ways.

In a recent interview to Geo TV former Pakistan Prime Minister Nawaz Sharif raised a storm in the country by denoting that Pakistan was a "failed state". While many would classify only countries as Somalia as a failed state, others may not be generous enough towards Pakistan as the elected governments since the 1990s have lost control. Non state actors have been dictating policy and these have been encouraged by the army. The problem is not that the political parties were not aware of this but were not willing to challenge the forces holding the strings as they were afraid of losing power.

Writing in the Daily Times on 18 December, retired Lt General Talat Masood a balanced observer of the domestic situation in the country is skeptical of the possibilities of success in dismantling the terrorist infra structure. He states,

> "Demobilisation of these groups is a huge challenge, and will require adroit handling. Merely banning these militant organisations will not make them disappear. In fact, they would simply go underground and pose an even greater threat. The Jama'at-ud Dawa ostensibly has an extensive social services network whose tasks the government and other benign NGOs will have to take up. Most importantly, the militants will have to be demotivated and rehabilitated by providing them alternate means of livelihood".[27]

The survey above would denote that a deeply entrenched terrorist network with global linkages will be difficult to dismantle in the near term even if the Pakistan government has the will and the Pakistan Army the capacity to do so. Sadly both have neither, thus indicating a long struggle before the terrorism as a tool for negotiation is removed from the policy discourse in South Asia.

## The Dilemma Before India

Given the deep roots of terrorism with spreading global tentacles, the International community and not just India is challenged by Pakistan. Noted analyst and author Ahmed Rashid sees the post Mumbai fault lines between India and Pakistan as a strategic opportunity to make peace if both countries understand the Al Qaeda game plan thus, "If India and Pakistan can understand that they are both victims of a strategic diversion by al-Qaeda and if international mediation can help deepen that understanding, then there is perhaps a greater opportunity for the two countries to address the conflicts that have bedevilled their relationship for 60 years - Kashmir and other lesser issues".[28]

Rohan Gunaratna speaks in much the same voice and states, "Over time, both New Delhi and Islamabad are likely to realize that they need to fight a common threat, both ideologically and operationally. Mumbai has demonstrated that the pre-eminent national security challenge facing both India and Pakistan is terrorism and not each other".

Pakistan's role in Kashmir given the response of the people of the state to elections is now limited and the coercive brand of separatism fostered by these groups have restricted relevance. At the same time there is willingness of both sides for greater openness to resolve the Kashmir issue with border trade having started thereby indicating that resolution through talks is feasible.

Under the circumstances terrorist groups as the LeT can be abandoned by the state. But this would have to be a gradual response for the public opinion in the country at present would not accept the government doing so as these are being wrongly tagged as nationalist forces. More over the Pakistan Army has to be amenable to overcoming its stranglehold on national security strategy which sees terror as a tool for caliberating not just relations with India but also the United States and the international community. Terror is thus seen ironically as a, "milking cow" through which American and international aid and assistance flows in. That much of this money goes in building up the army's conventional capabilities with massive seepages in corrupt networks has not prevented the inflow, such is the nuanced approach followed by the Pakistan General Headquarters based in Rawalpindi.

But there are hopes as a recent Gallup poll denoted, the Pakistani people want a crack down on terrorists.[29] Transforming internal resentment against terrorism is one option, just as the people of Mumbai forced New Delhi to accept that its path of countering terror in India was flawed. Ideally political leadership in Pakistan should lead the way, take the cue from the masses and join up to break decades long stranglehold of the Army on strategic policy. As former Prime Minister Nawaz Sharif has said most recently, the Charter of Democracy signed between him and late Benazir Bhutto in May 2006 provides a way to restructure Indo Pakistan and Indo Afghan relations presently held hostage to the warped theory of, "strategic depth". Para 17 of the Charter thus states, "Peaceful relations with India and Afghanistan will be pursued without prejudice to outstanding disputes".[30]

Thus a fundamental shift in Pakistan's policy is essential along with dominance of the strategic space by political government which can give a firm direction to the Army to clamp down on terrorism both within and without and the ISI its nefarious activities in India and Afghanistan. That such a direction was being followed by the PPP government was evident with the ISI's internal political division not being allotted any work recently. But Mumbai 26/11 may well delay transformation, for a shift in external intervention we need a resolute and unified political government in Islamabad. Till such time, which may well take many more years or even decades, Pakistan will continue to spawn terrorist groups which are motivated and trained for more Mumbai's in Delhi, Bangalore, Hyderabad, Jaipur, Ahmedabad, Surat and Varanasi if not London, Paris and New York.

---

**(Endnotes)**

1 LeT is looking at India through the global lens. The Sunday Times of India. 28 December 2008. New Delhi. P 18.

2 Nirupama Subramanian. Crackdown on Office of Lashkar's front organization. The Hindu 8 October 2008. New Delhi. P 1.

3 Militants have power to start regional war: Zardari. Khaleej Times Report. Available at http://www.khaleejtimes.ae/DisplayArticle.asp?xfile=data/mumbaiterror/2008/December/mumbaiterror_December7.xml&section=mumbaiterror&col=

4 Ibid.

5 Nirupama Subramanian. Pakistan : Between the rock and a hard place. The Hindu. 6 December 2008.New Delhi. P 10.

6 Asim Yasin. Mumbai blasts. Available at http://www.thenews.com.pk/ top_story_detail.asp?Id=18834

7 Muhammad Najeeb. No troop build-up on border with India: Pakistan military. Available at http://www.hindustantimes .com / StoryPage/ StoryPage.aspx?sectionName=MostPopular &id=197e3d0d-3614-46b1-a5df-9ad21a942308&&Headline=      No      +troop+build-up+on+border+with+India%2c+says+Pak+Army

8 Pakistan army vows peace amid tensions with India.  Available at http://www.hindustantimes.com/StoryPage/ FullcoverageStoryPage.aspx?id=ef7d27cd-5c3d-4b13-907a-badf98dd4566Mumbaiunderattack_Special&&Headline=Pakistan +army+vows+peace+amid+tensions+with+India

9 Anwar Iqbal. Pakistan not moving troops from Afghan border: US. Available at http://www.dawn.com/2008/12/06/top5.htm

10 Hamid Mir. Army official calls Baitullah Mehsud, Fazlullah 'patriots'. Available           at           http://www.thenews.com.pk/ top_story_detail.asp?Id=18709

11 Aakar Patel. The loneliness of Man Mohan Singh. Available at http:/ /www.thenews.com.pk/print1.asp?id=150625

12 Ibid.

13 Daily Times Editorial: Pakistan's institutional war continues. Available          at          http://www.dailytimes.com.pk/ default.asp?page=2008\12\06\story_6-12-2008_pg3_1

14 After India, Sharif slams Zardari, says Kasab from Pak. Available at http://www.expressindia.com/latest-news/After-India-Sharif-slams-Zardari-says-Kasab-from-Pak/400494/

15 Pak Army chief 20th most powerful person in world. Available at http://www.dnaindia.com/report.asp?newsid=1215987

16 K Subrahmanyam. Don't March to Their Beat. Times of India 3 December 2008. New Delhi. P 18

17 Hussain Haqqani. The ideologies of South Asian jihadi groups. Available at http://www.carnegieendowment.org/files/ideologies.pdf

18 Ibid.

19 Ibid.

20 LeT is looking at India through the global lens. The Sunday Times of India. 28 December 2008. New Delhi. P 18.

21 Ayaz Amir  Indian tragedy, Al-Qaeda triumph. Available at http://www.thenews.com.pk/daily_detail.asp?id=150622

22 Ibid.

23 Ahmed Rashid. Are Mumbai attacks a chance for peace? Available at http://news.bbc.co.uk/2/low/south_asia/7764475.stm

24 Ayaz Amir  Indian tragedy, Al-Qaeda triumph. Available at http://www.thenews.com.pk/daily_detail.asp?id=150622

25 Fred Burton and Ben West, in Stratfor.com report, "From the New York Landmarks Plot to the Mumbai Attack". Report shared by email to the author by Stratfor.com

26 Russian intelligence sees al Qaeda link to Mumbai attacks. Available at http://aajtv.com/news/World/123048_1detail.html

27 Talat Masood  In our own interest. Available at http://www.dailytimes.com.pk/default.asp?page=2008\12\18\story_18-12-2008_pg3_2

28 Ahmed Rashid. Are Mumbai attacks a chance for peace? Available at http://news.bbc.co.uk/2/low/south_asia/7764475.stm

29 Gallup poll shows public support for crackdown on terrorists. Available at http://www.dailytimes.com.pk/default.asp?page=2008\12\18\story_18-12-2008_pg1_3

30 Text of the Charter of Democracy. Available at http://www.dawn.com/2006/05/16/local23.htm

# 9

# Countering Terrorism - The Way Ahead

*"We cannot afford a repetition of the kind of terrorist attacks that have recently taken place in Delhi, Hyderabad, Bangalore, Mumbai, Ahmedabad, Surat, Guwahati and some other urban centers".*

Prime Minister Manmohan Singh to Director Generals of Police
on 23 November – three days before the Mumbai attacks.

## General

India's vulnerability to terror is becoming a national liability. The increased exposure to terrorist attacks is evident by the number of deaths in the past few years. In 2006, 271 people fell to terrorist violence; the figure went down to 152 in 2007 and for the current year till November stands at 377. On the other hand for an 11 year period from 1994 to 2005 the figure stood at 324. This excludes casualties in Jammu and Kashmir.[1] A nation regarded as a rising regional and global power is suffering from credibility because of its inability to successfully deal with the menace of terror. While we have effectively dealt with major challenges as the tsunami, earthquakes and are coping with the current financial meltdown, our ability to survive the next terror strike remains suspect. Such a situation if allowed to persist would impact our growth prospects as already India is being classified by some agencies as amongst the 20 most dangerous places to visit. Given that the service sector has a major role in our growth story, such a tag is best avoided and has to be shed at the earliest.

The response of the Indian state to the terror challenge is commonly believed to be ineffective. Mumbai is just a symbol of a larger malaise where inefficiencies in governance, policing and general administration have all contributed to the demand and supply factors that give rise to terrorism. While there has been an awareness that something should be done, given that terrorism was the theme of the Director General Police Conference held by the Ministry of Home Affairs on 23 November, just three days before the Mumbai attack, implementation remains a matter of concern.

Thus far the government had not been willing to acknowledge that there were deficiencies and the Centre was focused on passing the buck to the states, as is seen from the main thrust of then Home Minister Mr Shivraj Patil's speech during the DGP's Conference on 23 November where he has been quoted as saying, "Speaking at length about the measures required to be taken to counter terrorism, the Union Home Minister stressed the need for full and timely utilization of funds given by the Centre, filling up vacancies in the *State* police forces, preparation of plans to provide special security arrangements for cities, training of police forces in dealing with possible use of nuclear, biological and chemical devices, etc. by terrorists, appointment of a nodal officer in each *State* to ensure cooperation among *States* to control terrorism, and strengthening of special branches in the *States*" (Italics added by author).[2] The role of the Centre is seen as provision of funds and grandfathering state responses. The public outcry after Mumbai strikes for the first time resulted in the government accepting that there was an error and security had failed. Thus within a few days after taking over, Union Home Minister P Chidambaram conceded that there were lapses in Mumbai, "I agree that security and intelligence failed," said Chidambaram.

### Counter Terrorism Response to Mumbai

Taking the Mumbai episode, it would be seen that India's first responders, the local police were seen to be weak in Mumbai thereby providing an opportunity for the small group of terrorists to kill many and also lodge themselves in five star hotels where due to the layered nature of the rooms, search was difficult. Israeli media in particular was critical of the approach by the Indian responders. The Haaretz was reported by the Times of India as stating, "The first forces sent to the scene were inexperienced police officer, who suffered many casualties as a result". The Jerusalem Post was critical of the aspect that intelligence was not collected, "Indian forces were well trained but failed to collect sufficient intelligence before engaging the terrorists... and first taking control of the area".[3] There were thus large gaps observed in arming and equipping the police, their response to emergency situations and incident management.

The initial response of the NSG to the call for Mumbai has also come up for criticism as it took nine and half hours to reach the location due to lack of dedicated aircraft at its disposal and poor mobilisation procedures.[4] Why an aircraft on the runway in New Delhi of a public or private airlines company could not be commandeered under emergency circumstances remains unexplained. It is evident that the Crisis Management Group which can order such moves had not been activated. More over the IL 76 is a slow moving plane thus taking three hours to land in Mumbai against normal flying time of 1 hour 50 minutes or so for commercial aircraft. Quick Reaction teams are now being put into place with the Capital New Delhi leading to take immediate action on launch. This is essential to ensure that the response is timely.

India's counter terror infra structure has been under scrutiny for long with fragmentation of anti-terror efforts of the Central and State intelligence and police agencies. Political consensus has also been missing with no joint meeting held for a federal anti-terror agency and exploration of all possible models to tackle the menace of criminal or extremist terrorism until we faced 26/11 in Mumbai. The key problems with Indian counter terror philosophy and response could be summarized as follows:-

- Lack of political consensus.
- Synergy of effort through a unifying doctrine.
- Inability to differentiate response for counter insurgency and terrorism.
- Coordination of intelligence.
- Effective operational utilization of intelligence to prevent episodes.
- Lack of adequate counter terror capability of police forces.
- Poor incident management.
- Poor investigative capacities.
- Long winded judicial processes.

On its part the Central government was alive to the threat and has proposed a number of measures to overcome the debilities. The Prime Minister in the DGP Conference on 23 November sought to nominate a Task Force with a time bound 100-day plan under the National Security Adviser to undertake the following:-

- Develop an integrated capability to address emerging challenges in areas such as Left Wing Extremism, Terrorism and Insurgency;
- Improve the ability to anticipate and prevent surprises, through closely networked intelligence collaboration and up-gradation of both human and technological intelligence;
- Create an awareness regarding the critical importance of strategic foresight in regard to social and political developments;
- Develop a net-centric information command structure that enables both State and Central agencies to access and exploit information in a secure manner and well in time;
- Strengthen inter-State and inter-agency cooperation;
- Ensure innovation and technological leadership.[5]

The Lashkar e Taiyyaba, alas was not so generous as to offer this leeway of a 100 days, even as the Prime Minister and the Home Minister were addressing the DGPs, the Lashkar team under the leadership of Imran was heading for Mumbai. It struck three days later. Post Mumbai in a detailed statement in the Lok Sabha on 11 December 2008, the new Union Home Minister Mr P Chidambaram highlighted some of the measures being taken on priority basis to include the following[6 &7]:-

- A federal investigation agency with special powers to look into inter state crimes with international ramifications such as terrorism, drug trafficking and money laundering.
- Creation of Coastal Command under the Coast Guard with back up support of the Indian Navy.
- New anti terror law with stringent provisions as recommended by the Administrative Reforms Commission.
- Regional NSG hubs for real time response.
- Air defence measures to prevent a 9/11 type of terror strike by rogue or hijacked aircraft.
- Strengthening the intelligence network to include increase in the staff strength of the Intelligence Bureau and activating the Multi Agency Centre of the Intelligence Bureau.
- Establishment of 20 counter insurgency and anti terrorism schools.
- Two companies of India Reserve Battalions raised in States to be converted to special commando units for which additional assistance will be provided for training, and equipment by the government.

Some of these measures such as a stringent anti terror law and a federal investigation agency were being debated over the years, but no decisive action was taken. However the Mumbai strike has provided the necessary impetus driven by a younger and goal oriented Home Minister, Mr P Chidambaram and a new National Investigation Agency Bill has been passed by the Parliament which is included as Appendix A. Other proposals such as establishment of a Coastal Command and counter insurgency schools would have to be thought through in greater detail. Key issues such as coordination and decision making in the bureaucratic hierarchy of the government remain unaddressed. Counter terrorism specialists as Ajai Sahni Executive Director of the Institute for Conflict Management, one of the leading institutes on counter terrorism in South Asia comments on the measures instituted by the government thus, "It can be said, however, that most of these are, at best, marginally incremental, and, at worst, entirely misdirected". He also cites problems in implementation based on past performance, "While the various initiatives and sanctions announced can, at best, help in marginally augmenting capacities, it also remains the case that their implementation is, itself, suspect, given the Government's past record".[8]

In the final analysis, effective security and response mechanism at home and sustained pressure on Pakistan to part with the path of fundamentalism and dismantle the terror network remains the key to securing India from another terrorist strike. The way ahead on three critical issues intelligence, border and maritime security and police capability building is discussed as per succeeding paragraphs. The diplomatic response has been covered in other chapters including escalation-de-escalation model for India and Pakistan.

**Intelligence – Sustained Debility**

Four major terrorist attacks have occurred in India's financial capital Mumbai in the last 15 years as per chronology given below:-

• Nov 26 - 28, 2008: 172 killed and hundreds injured
in terror attacks in South Mumbai.
• July 11, 2006: 187 killed in seven blasts on suburban
trains and stations.
• Aug 25, 2003: 46 people killed in two blasts including
one near the Gateway of India.
• March 12, 1993: A series of bomb blasts left 257 dead
and around 700 injured. Buildings attacked included the
Bombay Stock Exchange, hotels, theatres, passport office,
Air India building and Sahar Airport.[9]

The Gateway of India has been targeted once before on 25
August 2003, thus should have been a high priority area for
surveillance and deployment of armed police force if not a counter
terrorist one.  There were also enough indicators that Mumbai
could be possibly next on the terror radar. Fahim Ansari alias
AbuZarar arrested in the Rampur Terror attack in UP case on 31
December 2007 had informed the police during interrogation that
the Lashkar was planning operations in Mumbai. He had been
tasked to carry out reconnaissance of Mumbai and had prepared
maps of the city. He had also prepared a target list such as the
Bombay Stock Exchange, Police Commissioner's Office and
Gateway of India.[10]

Intelligence or the lack of it is an issue which has been
discussed many times over. There is an impression supported by
even high ranking police officers in the country that countering
terrorism is a grass roots problem. While beat policing is
important, unless penetration of terrorist groups is carried out,
gaining intelligence of impending operations is not impossible.

Given that some of these groups are based outside the country, this will have to be a cloak and dagger operation, so be it.

Inability of agencies to penetrate groups within the country remains inexcusable. Premier intelligence agencies have been accused of focusing on collecting political rather than terror or criminal intelligence. Capacities of these agencies have to be build up through recruitment, adaptation and training. UK exponentially enhanced counter terror intelligence capability of the MI 5 after the London bombings through open recruiting a model which the IB could well follow.

Operationalising intelligence is another part of the same problem. Misled by the police brass some top political leaders in the country have stated that terror warnings are like weather bulletins. The inability of the local police to convert terror advisory into preventive actions on the ground is a gaping hole in our policing abilities which needs to be set right. Further more contribution and cooperation of citizens can be obtained by the simple tool of colour based advisories, red, amber, yellow and so on, which are common place in the West. A detailed perspective on operationalising intelligence to prevent terror attacks is thus felt essential and is as per succeeding paragraphs.

**Opertionalising Intelligence to Prevent Terrorist Attacks**

A terrorist attack would fall into the category of a, "known unknown", whereas normally in India it is believed to be an, "unknown unknown", using the famous phrase of Donald Rumsfield, former United States Secretary of Defence. While intelligence and information in some form is available, a key problem faced in countering terrorism is of operationalising intelligence. Intelligence warnings have been critiqued by many as vague and more or less like, "weather bulletins". Intelligence organizations in the country have thus been at the receiving end from time to time, be it the intrusion in Kargil in 1999, the attack on the Indian Parliament on 13 December 2001, the Indian embassy bombing in Kabul or the most recent Mumbai terror strike. While there are many short comings in intelligence coordination in the country, wherein most recipients feel that information is insufficient or so fuzzy that it is unactionable by the operating agencies, the police, security organisations and others, intelligence agencies have constantly refuted this claim. What ever is the case, operationalising intelligence remains a key challenge for countering terrorism in the country and the issue needs to be addressed on priority.

### Failure of Operationalisation of Intelligence – Mumbai 26/11

Much has been written and spoken about the Mumbai 26/11 terror attacks. Reports emanating in the media indicate that there were sufficient warnings of a terror strike at the precise targets where these actually occurred in South Mumbai and hotels such as the Taj. There are now enough indications that the warnings of an attack in Mumbai had been received from a number of different agencies and sources, some of which are summarized herein. Praveen Swami, writing in Weekly Assessments & Briefings of South Asia Terrorism Portal of 15 December 2008 indicates that the US Central Intelligence Agency (CIA) had provided two warnings of a possible attack on targets in Mumbai in locations which were frequented by foreigners. The Taj Mahal Hotel figured in the warning. The first such indication was provided on 18 September and the second on 24 September. The report by the CIA is presumed to be based on the movement of the Lashkar suicide attackers from Muridke to Karachi.[11]

The Indian Intelligence Bureau had also warned during the same period that LeT operatives had conducted several reconnaissance in the city of Mumbai.   Based on these warnings the Mumbai police are reported to have briefed top management of the Taj Mahal hotel and the Oberoi on the likely threat, while pamphlets were issued to shop and store owners seeking a high level of alertness and reporting of untoward movement in the area. The exact contents of the pamphlet could not be accessed.[12] A popular belief is that the first strike was to occur on 27 September but was postponed for reasons which are not clear at present. Would it be that one of the causes was the high level of alert issued by the Mumbai police based on these warnings to the business community, thereafter which precautions were taken but were later relaxed after lapse of time? Mumbai's vulnerability to an attack was also evident during interrogation of Ahmed Ansari a Lashkar operative who had reportedly provided details of training and planning of an attack on the commercial capital.

Coming on to the month of November 2008, Indian external intelligence agency, Research and Analysis Wing (RAW) had intercepted a phone conversation from a boat, the al Hussaini, on 18 November indicating that a 'consignment' was being transported to Mumbai. The RAW immediately passed on the information to the Indian Coast Guard and the Navy and on 20

November the Coast Guard is reported to have launched a search operation for the al Hussaini based on the coordinates provided by RAW.[13]

The Indian Express has given details of the warning received by the Coast Guard at the Jakhau station off the Bhuj coast. The Deputy Commandant of the station Mr Neelkanth M Yengde is reported to have warned the BSF commandant at Bhuj as well as the Commander of the Coast Guard Gujarat, Diu and Porbandar districts. He also diverted Hovercraft H 185 and off shore patrol vessel C 142 from the Tatraksha XXIV exercise due to operational requirements.[14] This search apparently ended on 21 November for reasons which remain unclear at present.

Another report by the Indian Express on 15 December indicates that the Indian Navy's Principal Director Naval Intelligence had received intelligence inputs of a Lashkar vessel with coordinates sailing under suspicious circumstances but did not share the same with the operational headquarters Western Naval Command.[15] Even the Coast Guard in Gujarat did not find it prudent to share the input with the Western Naval Command. While it may be conjectural at this stage but given that the Western Naval Command was conducting a live exercise of intrusion in the coastal area which involved searching of a large number of fishing vessels, passage of this vital input could have led to diversion of extensive resources deployed for this exercise to locate errant vessels as al Hussaini and possibly even MV Kuber on which the terrorists finally traveled to Mumbai.[16]

Tata group Chairperson Mr Ratan Tata accepted as much

that the Mumbai police had warned the Hotel that a terror strike was imminent and the Hotel had taken sufficient precautions, however the terrorists entered through the back door which was not protected.

There has been much debate about the possibilities of such strikes from Pakistan based group, Lashkar – E – Taiyyaba (LeT), the threat of infiltration from the sea and so on. The Lashkar – E – Taiyyaba [LeT] as is well known by now has expanded its overall aim from seeking accession of Jammu and Kashmir in Pakistan to pan Indian Jihad extending on to union of all Islamic countries around Pakistan to include Central Asia.[17&18.] The threat arising from the Lashkar has been discussed in Chapter 4 in detail. The LeT and its associates and collaborators and not a state actor are India's greatest enemy. Suffice to say that any intelligence warning of an attack by the LeT should have been taken as one of highest priority for it is an organisation comprising of motivated leadership with a well developed recruiting and training network, resources and support of the state to carry out its activities against India.

That Pakistan based terrorist groups were using the sea routes increasingly was clear. Given that the border fencing on the Indo Pakistan border has been completed and infiltration of Line of Control is becoming increasingly difficult with tiered surveillance by the army and an electronic blanket, the sea route was an option used particularly for high level well trained operatives and landing of large shipments of arms and explosives. One such consignment was reportedly landed on the coast of Maharashtra for an operation in Gujarat which was however aborted.[19] Another plot was successfully penetrated by the IB wherein eight Lashkar which landed off the Mumbai coast on March 3, 2007 were intercepted while operating in Jammu and Kashmir.[20]

Investigation of the serial bomb blasts in New Delhi on 13 September have also highlighted that the tragedy could have been averted only if the police had effectively decoded conversations of the cell phone of Mohammad Atif Ameen, leader of the Indian Mujahideen module that was behind the blasts. The purport of the conversation intercepted by the police was not immediately evident as the calls were not effectively analysed. It is only at the investigation stage on deliberate examination of the intercepts that a conspiracy was unraveled.[21] This once again highlights inadequacies in effective utilization of intelligence inputs for preventive measures.

A survey of the details of the above incidents would reveal some salient flaws in operationalising intelligence. While it is accepted that these deductions are from hindsight, their importance for future planning and dissipation of threats cannot be undermined and are as follows:-

- First and foremost, the threat by the Lashkar to India in general and in this case to Mumbai in particular was never taken seriously. Possibly it was not appreciated after the recent diversion of attention to terror strikes by the Indian Mujahideen that the LeT would continue to expand its, "war" against India beyond Kashmir. The fact that this threat is not episodic but long term and will manifest in a sustained manner has not been appreciated so far despite many past incidents of involvement of the LeT and open pronouncements by the Chief, Hafeez Sayeed of war against the Indian state. The Pakistan based group has spawned clones in India as the Indian Mujahideen. These would be all the more difficult to detect and identify given that they have the, "sea" of population to support them in the future.

• Operationalising the maritime threat in real time was not effective despite clear notice, again possibly these warnings were considered to be merely precautionary in nature and manifestation of terror attack was not considered realistic. This is evident from the Naval Headquarters not passing on vital inputs to Western command or the local Coast guard not passing the same laterally to the Navy. The search operation launched by Jakhau Coast commander was also not followed up to a logical conclusion to locate the errant ship given that the threat was considered marginal.

• Repeated warnings from intelligence and interrogation reports of a terror strike on Mumbai were not heeded. While in the last instance after the September warnings some action was taken, this was not followed up either by the Mumbai police or the hotel authorities, thinking that the threat had possibly passed away. More over Mumbai has been vulnerable to terror for a long period. Despite the same there is limited acceptance of this vulnerability in the masses which has possibly created a window of opportunity for the terrorist group.

- Detailed threat analysis of possible mode and manner of attack given that it included the maritime dimension, leading on to hotels in South Mumbai was also not apparently carried out. Had this been done, the jetty at Badhwar Park could have been placed under surveillance and locals warned to indicate landings to the police at the earliest. An informer network along the coast would have also proved valuable.

- The Mumbai police apparently did not appreciate the nature and types of attacks within the realms of possibility. In due fairness, to them, the technique of assault was highly unexpected but given that there is a sufficiently armed contingent in the city particularly in Chhatrapati Shivaji Terminal including the Railway Police Force, reactions and responses could have been better coordinated and rehearsed.

- Detailed analysis of all intercepts of vital investigations is essential. For this a pool of experts including technical and language would be required and normal police interrogation would not suffice. This requirement was also evident in Mumbai when the Maharashtra police had difficulty in deciphering the lone terrorist apprehended, Kasab's confessions as he spoke in native Punjabi prevalent in Southern Punjab Pakistan, alien to the primarily Marathi speaking police in Mumbai.

## Operationalisation – A Situation Based Model

To overcome failures of operationalising intelligence as brought out in the foregoing paragraphs a situation based model to highlight what steps can and should be taken at every level to ward off a strike is envisaged. As is evident from the incident of Mumbai and related episodes there were sufficient indications that the terror attack was likely at the stated location in South Mumbai. At the national level, our philosophy should be to preempt state and non state actors once warnings of such attacks have been received rather than accusing them later. Thus for instance had the government announced publicly that there were intelligence inputs of a LeT attack on Mumbai on say 20 November, raised the issue with Pakistan, knowing fully well that the group is based there, in all probability the mission would have been aborted by the perpetrators. In extreme cases options of targeting such groups inside Pakistani territory would have to be exercised rather than losing 200 innocent lives. Our weapons of war, such as surveillance and targeting assets are adequate for this purpose and need to be now employed in a terror scenario.

At times it may be possible that agencies giving such information, their means and techniques may get compromised. Another argument against it is that of a false alarm at a national level may embarrass us internationally given that such reactions are seen to be based on hypothetical inputs. However in the security environment in which we are placed these should be seen as standard practices where the rate of failure of warning denotes success rather than deficiency in the system. More over the losses incurred in the cautionary phase would be more than made up by avoiding terror attacks.

Internally on receipt of a warning, a public advisory should be issued so that the masses at large are made aware of the threat, are fully prepared and the support systems of the law and order machinery geared to meet the challenge. Had such a warning being issued in Mumbai on 18 September and then followed up on 20 November, the response could well have been different. While warnings were issued to the Coast Guard and perhaps other agencies a public warning in Mumbai given that the anticipated attack was expected there would have saved many lives.

There are considerable apprehensions in some quarters that such warnings create panic, depress business and particularly tourism. Instances of foreign governments issuing advisories to their citizens and causing unnecessary alarm have been quoted. These arguments are facetious. Security advisories are a standard practice in all developed nations and we should not shy away from bringing reality to the light of our public. This is an era of information sharing where the ordinary man is also sufficiently aware as to why a warning is being given. Such an advisory can be in the form of a colour code as is prevalent in many countries. Thus for instance the colour code for Mumbai on 20 November could have been raised to Red, a simple measure which would have put its citizens and police on the alert, saved many lives and losses apart from shattering the sense of security in the people.

The information provided by the intelligence agency also should be followed up till scope of any possible attack emanating from the thread of input is eliminated. Here there is a need for a high quality of analysis by specialists. If the Delhi conversation intercepts were wholly analysed and remedial actions taken, these would have possibly prevented the bombings on 13 September. Full scale analysis of citing of the Al Hussaini would have possibly led to the conclusion of a possible target and therefore interception of the boat on the long route to Mumbai would have been possible. Leaving leads half way has grave consequences. Again the pitfalls are the many, "wolf calls", but this is one of the accepted hazards in intelligence operations where every wolf call should be regarded as a success rather than a failure.

Action taken reports on intelligence inputs also need to be introduced. If the Coast Guard has given up the search the next day of receipt of input, this should have been questioned at an appropriate level and sufficient explanations asked rather than leaving it to the operational commander to call off the activity. Obviously the intelligence agency does not have sufficient confidence or is not fully empowered to carry out checks for this purpose. Since intelligence and operational responsibilities are generally concentrated under one head at a very senior level, even at the ministerial particularly at the centre where there is no operational head of the police, this failing is particularly noticeable. Central intelligence agencies need to be empowered to seek follow up of their inputs from the operational authorities to ensure that action is not left half way. Again the hazards would be apparent creating inter agency acrimony, but would have to be accepted in the interest of ensuring safety of the citizen.

On receipt of an intelligence input at each level, state, division and district, a detailed analysis of the same is essential to identify the who, when, where and how would the threat manifest. There is a frequent grouse that intelligence inputs are vague, though in Mumbai, the specific threat, Taj Hotel was identified. It should be remarked here that terrorist would want to gain maximum mileage from their attacks. Thus they are likely to strike targets such as religious places, bazaars, courts and government offices and so on. A detailed appreciation and vulnerability analysis is required to be carried out for each area or town separately which would ensure short listing of probable locations leaving ambiguity over when and how, which can be overcome by measures explained subsequently. Each district in particular would have already prepared a list of vulnerabilities and plan to counter a terrorist threat. On receipt of the threat this plan would be activated. Thus likely targets would be hardened, the routes to the same sanitized and the general level of alertness enhanced.

The informer network would have to be fully activated, communication monitoring enhanced, public nodes such as cyber cafes sensitized and a high level of information umbrella created down to the grass roots to ensure that any deviant activity is quickly processed and countered to avoid leading to an incident. Suspects including criminal elements would have to be rounded up if need be and for this purpose, there may be a necessity for tapping available laws and rules. The mafia networks operating in some areas of our country are a reality. The police is well aware of these groups and have links with them. These should also be activated to ensure that they are not supporting the terrorist group and if approached will provide information to the police.

At the sharp end is the beat policeman who will act not just as the eyes and ears but also an information node filtering inputs from the network of adhoc information providers, local tuck shop owners, hawkers and redi wallahs who are regulars and can provide details of unusual activity of personnel in the area. Intensity and frequency of beat policing would have to be enhanced particularly in the more sensitive areas.

Electronic and communication surveillance is an important facet of this exercise. Terrorist groups survive on communications. They would be using the internet, multiple sims and evasive means to ensure that they leave no trail. Legal provisions should be exercised to tap into communication networks and any new activity promptly observed and tracked. New sim numbers would have to be tracked to the source, thereby eliminating any possibility of being used by disruptive elements from outside.

Armed police sub units should be placed at selected location centrally or at vulnerable points to target the terrorists promptly and avoid the mayhem created at the Chhatrapati Shivaji Terminal in Mumbai where resistance offered was poor thereby resulting in the deaths of over 48 innocents. Trained armed police men firing even with weapons such as .303 would have brought down the terrorists, but no signs of such a resistance were seen.

Obviously the police force for such a purpose will never be adequate. Thus a priority based deployment would have to be undertaken to utilize the manpower most effectively. Networking with private security agencies would have to be carried out to make up for the shortfall.

In a bottom up approach then preparedness and emergency response should be tested so that emergency forces available from the district to the state to the national level are placed on the same grid. Such rehearsals have to include a wide variety of establishments as fire fighting squads and home guards. Establishment of incident command posts at each level is important and needs to be rehearsed. Assistance from the local military garrisons should also be sought and since this requires certain procedural issues, these need to be taped up. Even the incorporation of NSG and bomb squads would have to be thought through. Such rehearsals should be evaluated by superior authorities, feed back provided and glitches removed so that over a time a responsive reaction from the lowest to the highest is networked.

For effective response, apart from counter terrorist drills, local police would have to be trained to be physically fit, at employing fire arms and perform lathi drills. The lathi if used effectively is a most dangerous weapon, but for which training is essential. Age cannot be taken as an excuse for not undertaking physical exercises or routine arms firing which has to be mandatory. The entire range of activities related to an incident including procedures such as cordoning and sealing off areas also need to be practiced.

At the state and central level, the Director Generals of Police and ministers have to seek continuous feedback on the actions taken on the intelligence warnings. The golden principle being any thing that is not checked is assumed as not completed. Thus there is a need for reports on reaction of various agencies to the intelligence warnings which should be taken verbally as well as in writing to develop a high level of awareness and accountability.

Given the elaborate measures identified above, it is likely that the terrorist group would prefer not to strike a well guarded target when we are well prepared. Our aim is partially achieved. The problem now is to keep up the vigilance and be prepared the next time around when such a warning comes, for it would be difficult to sustain the interest of the police as well as the populace whose full cooperation is essential to prevent such incidents. Senior leadership would have to step in to explain to the rank and file the importance of preemptive actions and results achieved of keeping the area terror free. Each time an incident is avoided a reward system can be instituted so that interest is retained. Thus innovative measures would have to be employed to ensure that complacency is overcome and the response and reaction is improved successively.

## Institutional Measures to Support Operationalisation

Operational measures taken at the grass roots would have to be supported by institutional measures at the national and the state level. Some of these facets are elaborated as per succeeding paragraphs.

## Terrorism as an Existential Threat

Groups as the Lashkar e Taiyyaba have adopted the strategy of a hundred cuts to exercise influence over India and to create what was not possible post partition an Islamic rule across the Sub Continent. Frequently the state does not view this as an existential threat but merely an issue of law and order or an episodic one. This perception needs to change and terrorism has to be seen as an existential threat, for it is seen to impact first and foremost the lives of innocent citizens which the state is charged to protect. More over it is also impacting sovereignty, integrity and communal harmony of the nation. While the people at large of all communities have understood the sinister designs and will not fall prey to the type of rioting witnessed earlier, there are elements within a community who would be sufficiently moved to act against the people emotionally charged through acts of deviants. Thus it is important today to view terrorism as an existential rather than a marginal threat as this approach has only led to an increase in vulnerability of the country to terrorist strikes.

## Actualisation of Threat from Non State Actors to the Country

India has faced a threat from non state actors employing terror and waging a guerrilla war against the state for over 60 years now. There is recognition of this challenge. Thus the Prime Minister in his address to the Director Generals of Police Annual Conference on 23 November stated, "The advent of many non-state actors has greatly increased our vulnerabilities. Terrorism is now recognized as the main scourge of the modern world". So far there was a perception that these groups were largely indigenous and their scope geographically limited to their areas of interest. Expansion of the challenge to the country at large, its complex network which is seen to emanate from Muridke in

Pakistan to Mumbai has possibly not been fully appreciated. More over actualization of the threat from non state actors, by understanding its many dimensions and networked nature is not evident.

There is a need therefore to examine in totality non state actors across the globe who are ranged against the Indian state, include these in the groups banned under the Unlawful Activities Act even where these may not be resident in India and take diplomatic, overt and covert actions if required to effectively deter their activities and neutralize their threat. A cursory examination would reveal four prominent groups based outside India which pose a threat to the Indian state apart from the localized operations by others in Kashmir and the North East, these are the Jamaat ud Dawa-Lashkar e Taiyyaba, Jaish e Mohammad, the Harkat ul Jihadi Islam or HUJI based in Bangladesh and some other members of the International Islamic Front. A sustained effort is essential to identify and neutralize the challenge of these groups including their fostering Indian clones as the Indian Mujahideen. A realization must seep in that these groups are the new, "enemy" of the state and have to be tackled on an emergency basis. The focus of all arms of the state including the armed forces has to be to neutralize them.

Developing a deeper understanding of these groups and the manner in which they operate is important. Their use of criminal networks as the Dawood Ibrahim gang is well documented. The financial and hawala networks used are complimented by the regular businesses being run by criminal syndicates and money supply from trusts and endowments based in the Gulf. Sustained pressure focusing on each organization to include its leadership, financial, charity, endowment and other support networks is essential to keep them on the run and preventing free space for planning and execution such assaults as in Mumbai.

This threat is long term and thus measures also need to be taken to defeat the designs in a holistic manner over a period starting with what could be the immediate response to beat an attack which may emerge now to something which will occur in the future.

**Evolving a Counter Terrorism Doctrine**

Terrorism is an activity which involves a wide range of personnel, agencies and organizations at the cutting edge. This includes the highest office of the country to the common citizen of the street. It is extremely important that given the challenge faced each man must be able to perform a specific role and a function to defeat this challenge particularly till the capacity of our police forces is not sufficiently enhanced to target the terrorist groups in their lair. To bring every one on a common platform a doctrinal approach is essential which can lay down a framework for action by each individual in his own sphere of activity.

Another failing in this sphere is lack of distinction between terrorism and insurgency. This has led to applying principles of counter insurgency to terrorism with deleterious impact. Insurgency and terrorism may not be as different as chalk and cheese, but there are major nuances which necessitates differences in responding to both. A few months back it was evident that the Intelligence Bureau was working on such a document, but this has not seen the light of the day so far. Each aspect of counter terrorism needs to be covered in such a doctrine to draft which an agency needs to be nominated at the earliest.

**Intelligence Cooperation and Coordination**

The need for vertical and horizontal intelligence cooperation and coordination has been highlighted from time to time. This lacks effective implementation. Thus the Prime Minister addressing the Director Generals of Police Annual Conference on 23 November had amply brought out the need to improve the ability to anticipate and prevent surprises, through closely networked intelligence collaboration and up gradation of both human and technological intelligence; developing a net-centric information command structure that enables both State and Central agencies to access and exploiting information in a secure manner and well in time. [22]

Intelligence culture in the country so far has been that of controlled dissemination of information in the belief that withholding information is power. In the information environment of the future, sharing rather than holding back information is power and adequate mechanisms to ensure the same need to be evolved. One way out is to take assistance of information and communication technologies to provide simultaneous dissemination of information. Thus a country wide intelligence network covering the primary agencies both intelligence and executive would have avoided the bane that was in Mumbai.

## Inter State and Agency Cooperation

Given the complex administrative processes in the country with a federal structure, law and order is a state subject. As all police actions have to be accountable in law, there is considerable hesitation in exceeding the brief. The active human rights movement has to be lauded. However frequently this has become the reasons for police and intelligence officers failing to follow up lead when it goes beyond their own domain. The need for strengthening inter-State and inter-agency cooperation has already been highlighted by the Prime Minister in his speech of 23 November.[23] It is now creating mechanisms and organizations to implement this desire, with the National Investigation Act having been passed in the parliament, other mechanisms to integrate intelligence are essential.

## National Citizens Data Base

The proposal for a national identity card has been mooted from time to time; however the same has not been effectively implemented. It is surprising that the Election Commission which has perhaps far less resources than the central and state government has been able to issue a comprehensive electoral roll and election identity cards but the same has not been possible for the administration. Action to prepare national citizens data base with identity cards has to be completed on priority. This would enable tracking antecedents of every new individual in a locality most effectively and prevent infiltration and intrusions from outside. This will greatly facilitate the police even at the grass roots where all police stations would be networked on a single national grid to trace the antecedents of a new individual rather than relying on hearsay.

## Terrorism Research and Development

The failure to appreciate the type of attack which involved a complex operation and used multiple means of approach to the targets, assault, and use of bombs, indiscriminate automatic firing and hostage taking was evident in Mumbai. Thus far the standard techniques of attack in the hinterland have been serial bombs used extensively on a number of occasions. There was a lack of anticipation that such a strike will come in. There have been previous incidents of such terror attacks, but these have apparently not been studied. In an attack in the Red Fort in New Delhi in 2000 terrorists had used assault rifles and grenades. In Rampur near Bareilly on New Year 2008, the terrorists in a mid night attack had again used assault rifles. The right lessons were apparently not drawn and the type of attacks that they would launch was not envisaged.

Moreover India specific research on terrorism is lacking. Who will take such a project remains a question. Terrorism so far falls beyond the purview of the armed forces and also perhaps the police. Lying in the median ground, there is a need to nominate a body to undertake such research. The Bureau of Police Research could be one agency which may be found suitable. On the other hand the Indian Navy and the Coast Guard along with the marine police in the country need to carry out research in one of the many excellent institutions that the armed forces run on maritime terrorism. Institutional research would provide us adequate inputs into the future.

**Border and Coastal Security**

With multi dimensional threats from terrorism posed to the country, a holistic security response which covers border and coastal security is essential. The Mumbai incident highlighted the significance and gaps in coastal security, but there are other dimensions as with over 15,000 kms of land border, the challenges to secure our frontiers are many. According to former Home Minister Mr Shivraj Patil, the terrorists' game plan also included capturing un-inhabited islands off the country's coastline and using them as launching pads for terror strikes on oil refineries in coastal areas. "We understand they (terrorists) have been collecting information regarding location of various refineries on or near the Indian coastline," the minister had said adding that even shipyards and multi-purpose projects were targets. Maritime security would thus assume importance.

Surveillance of the 12 nautical miles off coastline is responsibility of the state marine police; the Coast Guard is responsible from 12 to 200 miles and the Indian Navy beyond that. Coordination of these forces is to be carried out and all gaps eliminated in case of a threat close to the shore.[24] The marine police all but exist on paper; the Coast Guard is short of boats to perform its task while the Indian Navy appears to have only now got into the grid of conducting low intensity maritime operations. (LIMO). The Ministry of Home Affairs (MHA) Status report dated

1 September 2008 claims that 55 of the 73 police stations are operational 22 of these as per the MHA Annual report in Maharashtra and Gujarat. A joint patrolling scheme Operation Swan has also been put into place for these two states in the third year of the five year plan starting 2005-06. The ease with which terrorists have been able to enter India's commercial capital indicates the lackadaisical approach with which this scheme has been implemented.

A National Maritime Commission to synergize security was planned in the past but was shelved has to be established. "We are pushing for a proper infrastructure to bring synergy among different agencies working in the maritime domain," said Navy chief Admiral Sureesh Mehta. The surveillance of the Indian Navy and the Coast Guard remains poor thereby allowing Pakistani boats and fishermen clear access to the seas. It is now proposed to create maritime defence zones (MDZs) integrating the Navy and Coast Guard. This will have a single commander and would enhance security of offshore oil assets, coastal waters and port security. "There could be, for instance, two to three MDZs each for the west and the east coast, apart from another one for the strategic Andaman and Nicobar Islands," a senior official was quoted by the Times of India in a report.[25] The Home Minister has also clarified that a coastal command with a mandate to ensure coastal security is to be set up.[26]

Formation of a Coastal command was long over due but the nature of its functioning to be probably divided into three to four maritime zones to cover the long coastal territory of the country would have to be formalized. Maritime defence zones within the command may have to therefore oversee security of the Eastern, the Southern and the Western sea board. The latter is the most vulnerable and hence maximum security resources would have to be deployed for securing the Gujarat and Maharashtra coast line, due to its proximity to Pakistan and also with a large number of strategic energy assets both on and off shore existing in the area. As a start point, it would be appropriate to task the Coastal Command to focus on the Western coast expanding its influence in other areas subsequently. The maritime police stations should also be prioritized on this coast line rather than spreading the same evenly across the country.

Some other measures suggested by the Indian Navy officials in the report include the following:-

- Fast tracking induction of 204 patrol boats for marine police forces approved under Coastal Security Scheme of March 2006.
- Increasing Coast Guard force-levels from the present 80 vessels and 45 aircraft to 106 vessels and 52 aircraft.
- Increasing training of marine police personnel by the Coast Guard from the present 1,000 trained so far.
- Induction of coastal radars, AIS (automatic identification system) transponders and other equipment for surveillance of the long 7,516-km coastline particularly on the Maharashtra and Gujarat coasts to cover areas 20-25 km from the coast.

Post Mumbai strike, the Ministry of Home Affairs is laying

additional emphasis on maritime security. In a conference held with key officials of nine coastal states and four union territories on 5 December a number of issues were coordinated. "The Home Secretary stressed that all the 73 Coastal Security Police Stations, 97 Check Posts and 58 Outposts should become fully operational within the shortest possible time. He also asked the States and UTs to be ready with adequate and trained manpower so that they can be fully and optimally utilized once the delivery of 204 Interceptor Boats commences from March-April 2009. In this regard, it is likely that the delivery may commence even earlier and that the total time span for delivery of all boats would also be compressed. He emphasized the need to finalise the deployment norms and the Standard Operating Procedures also to ensure operational efficiency and effectiveness", said the Press Release on the occasion.[27]

The meeting also considered other issues as Identity Cards to all fishermen and sea-faring personnel and for registration of boats and optimal use of technology for purposes of providing Transponders and Global Positioning Systems on the registered boats/vehicles and for issue of digitized identity cards. Given the slow pace in implementation of the Coastal Security Scheme launched in 2005-06, the large number of agencies involved and lack of systemic coordination of monitoring mechanisms a the Centre to ensure implementation, capacity building in this sphere will come about only with a sustained push at all levels, Centre, states and the Union Territories duly supported by organizations as the National Maritime Commission as and when formed. In the past the concept of border management was broad based with elements of Special Services

Bureau ensuring that the population supported the security forces and information and intelligence was generated from the grass roots. This model may have to be replicated in the coastal areas in the future.

Coastal security addresses only a part of the problem. India has 15106.7 Km of land border running through 92 districts in 17 States and a coastline of 7516.6 Km touching 13 States and Union Territories (UTs). India also has a total of 1197 islands accounting for 2094 Km of additional coastline. The length of India's land borders with neighbouring countries is as given below[28]:-

- Bangladesh    - 4096.7 Km
- China         - 3488 Km
- Pakistan      - 3323 Km
- Nepal         - 1751 Km
- Myanmar       - 1643 Km
- Bhutan        - 699 Km
- Afghanistan   - 106 Km
- Total         - 15106.7 Km

Security of such a vast stretch of land border and coast line with antagonist states such as Pakistan and those having poor control over the border areas as Myanmar and Bangladesh has to be managed with greater rigour. There are reports of the border fencing with Pakistan being sabotaged by smugglers by tunneling underground, movement of counterfeit currency is rampant while the open border between Nepal and India has been a constant source of concern due to free movement of criminal and other anti social elements of both countries.[29]

Then there are major gaps in the Indian Air Force capabilities to cover aerial threats from low level transportable radars which presently span only 24% of the actual requirement at heights up to 2000 metres.[30] We need to meet all these challenges to secure our borders and coast line from a vicious nexus of smugglers, terrorists, drug and people traffickers.

**Police Capacity Building – An Integrated Architecture**

Police modernisation and capacity building in India has engaged the security community for many years now. The present notion of modernisation is buying vehicles, communication equipment or at the most smart weapons for the elite. The government had sanctioned almost Rs 1000 Crore for police modernization but not much of the money has gone into up gradation of capacity at the grass roots to include buying of ammunition and training of the police, bullet proof jackets or other life saving gear.[31] The response of our bravest officers who sacrificed their lives as they went into encounters unprepared bears testimony to what needs to be done in the days ahead.

Training equipping, rehearsals and response management to tackle terrorist attacks should be a part of normal policing now rather than being the exclusive preserve of the NSG. Decentralisation of the NSG would also help but it should not hamper its training and command and control. More and more state police forces in the country have now started thinking of raising special counter terrorism forces on the pattern of the NSG.

Maharashtra state police plan to take the lead in setting up state level special forces teams. The state home minister Jayant Patil announced formation of such a force in the assembly. Mumbai police commissioner Hassan Gafoor wants this force to be exclusively from former army short service officers as he believes that the armed forces provide the grit and determination required for combating terrorists. Named as, Force 1 it is slated to have 142 posts with 60 reserved for ex army personnel. The age of the force at entry would be 28 years and special training would be carried out with the NSG. The force is slated to have an ambitious response time of three minutes.[32]

A critical component of policing is numbers. Despite additional allocations and emphasis of the central government on enhancing numbers by the states, it is evident that the police population ratio in India has gone down from 126 per 100,000 in 2006 to 125 in 2007. On the other hand police forces in developed countries have a much higher ratio of 225 per 100,000 to over 500 per 100,000.[33] However adequacy of numbers is no guarantee for successful counter terrorism. Manipur, a state in the North East chronically affected by terrorism boasts of a police population ratio of 554 per 100,000, yet incidents of extortion, kidnapping, grenade throwing in high security zones are common in Imphal, the capital. On the other hand Nagaland, which has a marginally higher ratio at 558 is considered a relatively safe state from the law and order point of view but is affected by inter group rivalry of militant groups which have ceased hostilities with state forces under Cease Fire Agreements.[34]

While numbers per se may not be the sole criterion, past

experience has shown that a security forces to population ratio of 2000 per 100,000 is essential for successfully countering insurgency. For instanee James T. Quinlivan a military analyst and senior mathematician at Rand quotes figures from British experience in Northern Ireland and Malaya to state that a ratio of about 20 security personnel including police and army per thousand inhabitants were deployed in these areas.[35] Realistic estimates of what is required for counter terrorism are not available, is it a median at 1000 per 100,000 of population or much the same to combat insurgency, suffice to say the present ratios of our police at 225 per 100,000 are not adequate to maintain law and order what to talk of countering terrorism.

Beyond numbers it is training, physical fitness and responsiveness of the police that would add to counter terrorism capabilities. Corruption not just in monetary terms but in maintaining standards of normal efficiency is rampant in the police force in India. No training is carried out worth its name after the initial period of induction by the police in the country. Thus arms are rusting; ammunition is expended sporadically by the select few, while physical fitness is low. The proverbial image of the Indian policemen is that of a potbellied constable constantly seeking gratification from his, "victims". Thus the police are pilloried in movies and television serials, a true reflection of their perception in society. It is therefore evident that along with numbers per se, quality of training and effective implementation is a key issue for the Indian police if they want to challenge the terrorist.

Beyond personnel numbers and training is the issue of

coordination. India has a plethora of local, state and central police and para military forces. Thus at any one time in a given area affected by militancy or terrorism a variety of police could be deployed, ranging from the home guards, local police, state armed police, Central Reserve Police Force, which also has a separate Rapid Action Force, Border Security Force, Indo Tibetan Border Police, India Reserve Battalion, National Security Guards, Assam Rifles and finally the army. Private security guards and agencies are another component of the security set up. Coordination between these multiple agencies on the ground is difficult, at the higher level it is virtually impossible despite formation of integrating mechanisms as the Unified Command in Kashmir and Assam.

Now with states raising NSG type of force such as the Force 1 proposed by the Maharashtra government, there may be more organizational chaos in the offing. What is required is a holistic appraisal of the police organizations, their stream lining and effective employment with nominated coordination agencies at each stage. More over when major incidents as Mumbai 26/11 happen, an incident command post has to be established by the local police at the site or as near as is possible from the communication point of view to coordinate all operations including control of the population and media briefings. These measures would facilitate enhancing the local response while channelising add-on forces in the desired operational direction.

With private corporations increasingly going in for their own security set ups as Ratan Tata, chairman of Tata Sons, announced recently, "We have decided that we will now look at anti-terrorism or protection of our assets and our people ourselves and we will try to create a deterrent. We will not try to create heroes who will engage in the enemy but to try and find as many invisible forms of deterring this, containing them or thwarting their efforts and that's what we are engaged in doing and we will seek external expertise to help us set it up," he said.[36] Private security establishments would no doubt add to capability of the police provided these are effectively integrated into an overall police architecture.

A National Investigation Agency is now being put into place. But this is not likely to solve the immediate problems of countering terrorism. Ajai Sahni commenting on the National Investigation Agency Bill states that past experience as well as functioning of such agencies in other states including Pakistan denotes that this has not been successful. He states, "What is argued here is not that the NIA can have no conceivable utility within the architecture of counter-terrorist strategy, but that it can have no immediate utility within the circumstances currently prevailing in India; that this cannot be a national priority; and that the NIA that India is currently capable of putting up (in terms of manpower, resources and skills) can have no plausible bearing on the trajectory of terrorism in India".[37] The NIA as per Sahni will impinge on the present organizational functioning rather than supplementing it thus, "The NIA can only cannibalize existing organisations – already suffering from acute skill and manpower shortages – for a small manpower component in the foreseeable future". These observations need to be examined in totality to ensure that in implementation the NIA Bill seeks to overcome the same so that the alacrity with which such a measure is taken fructifies into tangible counter terrorism gains on the ground.

**Conclusion**

Terrorist acts not with standing the popular notion cultivated by effete political leadership and the police are preventable. Using the theory of Power laws, frequency of incidents of terror in the country today is one major incident per month. The chronology going back from Mumbai on 26 November to Guwahati in October, Delhi September, Bangalore, Ahmedabad and Surat in July and Jaipur in May should prove the point.

Locating the next target is also not very difficult. The Indian Mujahideen had very clearly indicated as early as in July that the next strike would be Mumbai. Obviously the state and central government failed to take this threat seriously and build capacity of the police force to face this challenge. In the interim period the social capital in Mumbai post the insider-outsider controversy had greatly weakened. These were the makings of a soft target the perpetrators of terror were awaiting.

The challenge is also not insurmountable. Building political consensus on terrorism is the first requisite. Polarisation for votes is a natural process of electoral democracy. But there are red lines which political leaders need to draw and combating acts of terror or violent intimidation irrespective of religion, caste or creed is one frontier which cannot be breached.

Countering terrorism is thus a holistic process. To tackle

terror we need leadership. Hundreds of citizens who have lost
their lives in the recent past deserve political, police and
administrative leaders who are responsible and accountable for
their commissions and omissions and not just treat every incident
as another opportunity to shed crocodile tears. [38] All measures
identified above would fall short if we do not have leaders who
are willing to understand the nuance of new wave terror and are
determined to eliminate the same from the country.

Shedding the tag of a country vulnerable from terrorist
attacks is essential for India if it wants to rise above the mediocrity
of a developing country. While measures such as better
coordination of intelligence, National Investigation Agency, police
capability building, creation of specialist hubs and so on are being
taken, these are not adequate to prevent a terror strike. One facet
of the problem is that of operationalisation of intelligence. Training
and enhancing accountability would be the other components of
this same framework. Supervision of implementation is also
important, which has to come from the top. Thus by adopting a
top-down approach for supervision and a bottoms-up approach
for implementation, an effective counter terrorism grid can be
created. Once a successful cycle has been established, confidence
levels of the police will be raised and the terrorist groups deflated,
thereby establishing a positive spiral, making India terror free.
This should now be a national endeavour.

---

**(Endnotes)**

1 Times of India Report. Terror in Afghanistan, Pak Spilling over into
India. Times of India Report 5 December 2008. p 18.

2 States should train some forces for countering terrorism says Shivraj

Patil. PIB press release. Available at MHA.nic.in.

3 Israel Slams 'botched' response. Times of India Report. Times of India. 29 November 2008. New Delhi. P 17.

4 Times of India Report. Why did NSG take 9 hours to get there? Times of India Report 30 November 2008. p 1.

5 PM's address at the DGP's Conference. 23 November 2008. Available at http://pmindia.nic.in/speeches.htm.

6 HM announces measures to enhance security. Available at http://pib.nic.in/release/release.asp?relid=45446&kwd=

7 Indian Express Report. Broad Contours of the Government's Response. Indian Express. 12 December 2008. New Delhi. P 4.

8 Ajai Sahni. Strategic Vastu Shashtra. Weekly Assessments & Briefings
Volume 7, No. 24, December 22, 2008. South Asia Intelligence Review 7.24. Subscribed by E Mail by the author. See satp.org.

9 With inputs from Zee news Report. Major terror attacks in Mumbai: Timeline. Available at http://www.zeenews.com/nation/2008-11-27/486885news.html

10 Sanjay Singh and Manish Sahu. Fahim had forewarned about Mumbai attacks but no one listened. The Indian Express 6 December 2008. New Delhi. P 9.

11 Praveen Swami. Mumbai: The Road to Maximum Terror. Weekly Assessments & Briefings. Volume 7, No. 23, December 15, 2008. www.satp.org provided by E Mail subscribed to by the author

12 Ibid.

13 Ibid.

14 Shishir Gupta. Coast Guard Moved on Lashkar Alert but was all at sea. The Indian Express. 11 December 2008. New Delhi. P 1-2.

15 Ibid.

16 Ibid.

17 General Y M Bammi. War Against Insurgency and Terrorism in Kashmir. Natraj. Dehradun. 2007. p 95

18 Lashkar e Taiyyaba  Extension of Kashmir Jihad Factory. Unpublished paper by security-risks.com

19 Praveen Swami. Mumbai: The Road to Maximum Terror. Weekly Assessments & Briefings. Volume 7, No. 23, December 15, 2008. www.satp.org provided by E Mail subscribed to by the author

20 Ibid.

21 Smriti Singh. Rahul Tripathi. Delhi blasts could have been averted. Times of India. 18 December 2008. New Delhi. p 1

22 Prime Minister's address to the Director Generals of Police Annual Conference on 23 November. Available at http://pmindia.nic.in/ speeches.htm.

23 Prime Minister's address to the Director Generals of Police Annual Conference on 23 November. Available at http://pmindia.nic.in/ speeches.htm.

24 Maharashtra neglected marine security: C&AG report. Available at http://economictimes.indiatimes.com/News/PoliticsNation/ Maharashtra_neglected_marine_security_CAG_report/articleshow/ 3782525.cms

25 Rajat Pandit. Complete overhaul of coastal security setup needed. Available      at      http://timesofindia.indiatimes.com/India/ Complete_overhaul_of_coastal_security_setup_needed/articleshow/ 3789428.cms

26 HM announces measures to enhance security. Available at http:// pib.nic.in/release/release.asp?relid=45446&kwd=

27 Home Secretary reviews Coastal Security with concerned States & UTs.      Available      at      http://pib.nic.in/release/ release.asp?relid=45370&kwd=

28 Ministry of Home Affairs. Outcome Report. 2007-08. Available at

MHA.nic.in

29 Cops discover tunnel running from India to Pak. CNN IBN report 22 December 2008. Available at http://ibnlive.in.com/news/cops-discover-tunnel-running-from-india-to-pak/81129-3.html

30 Antony takes blame for air defence gaps. Press Trust of India Report. Available at http://www.ndtv.com/convergence/ndtv/story.aspx?id=NEWEN20080070074

31 Times of India Report. The Times of India. 1 December 2008. New Delhi. P 13.

32 Somit Sen. Once in the army, now in Force One. Times of India 20 December 2008. New Delhi. P 2.

33 Ajai Sahni. Strategic Vastu Shashtra. Weekly Assessments & Briefings

Volume 7, No. 24, December 22, 2008. South Asia Intelligence Review 7.24. Subscribed by E Mail by the author. See satp.org.

34 Bibhuti Prasad Routray. Nagaland: Epitome of police ineptitude. Available at http://www.nagalim.co.uk/article4124.html

35 James T. Quinlivan. Burden of Victory The Painful Arithmetic of Stability Operations. Available at http://www.rand.org/publications/randreview/issues/summer2003/burden.html

36 We'll create our own anti-terror mechanism: Tata. Times of India Report. Available at

http://timesofindia.indiatimes.com/India/Well_create_our_own_anti-terror_mechanism_Tata/articleshow/3848228.cms

37 Ajai Sahni. Strategic Vastu Shashtra. Weekly Assessments & Briefings

Volume 7, No. 24, December 22, 2008. South Asia Intelligence Review 7.24. Subscribed by E Mail by the author. See satp.org.

38 Some parts of this section were first published in an opinion piece in the Mint, New Delhi on 27 November 2008 by the author.

# *About The Author*

Brig Rahul K Bhonsle is a military veteran with over three decades of active service. He is now pursuing a second career in research and knowledge management at an independent agency, Security-risks.com which has established a niche for fast track research projects, papers, round tables, security advisories and briefings to military, academia and the corporate sector. His areas of interest include South Asia, future warfare and human security.

He is a regular contributor to leading main stream and professional newspapers, Web sites and Journals and edits a monthly, "South Asia Security Trends". He is presently working on Net Assessment of the Indian Armed Forces. He has authored aseries of books on South Asia namely, 'India Security Scope: The New Great Game' in 2006, 'South Asia Security Trends' in 2007 and 'South Asia - Political, Security and Terrorism Trends' in 2008 which have received favourable professional reviews. The author blends his professional military experience with academic exposure to provide realistic scenarios in the region distilled through interaction with a wide range of experts in the strategic community in South Asia from time to time.

www.ingramcontent.com/pod-product-compliance
Lightning Source LLC
Chambersburg PA
CBHW071051280326
41928CB00050B/2184